New Orleans

Berlitz Publishing Company, Inc.

Princeton   Mexico City   Dublin   Eschborn   Singapore

Text:	Lindsay Bennett
Editor:	Allison Greene
Photography:	Pete Bennett
Cover Photo:	Pete Bennett
Photo Editor:	Naomi Zinn
Layout:	Media Content Marketing, Inc.
Cartography:	Ortelius Design

Although the publisher tries to insure the accuracy of all the infor-
mation in this book, changes are inevitable and errors may result.
The publisher cannot be responsible for any resulting loss, incon-
venience, or injury. If you find an error in this guide, please let the
editors know by writing to Berlitz Publishing Company, 400
Alexander Park, Princeton, NJ 08540-6306.

ISBN 2-8315-7702-0

Printed in Italy
010/011 REV

CONTENTS

● A () in the text denotes a highly recommended sight

NEW ORLEANS AND
ITS PEOPLE

New Orleans, Louisiana is one of the most famous cities in the world. It's been praised in song, written about in numerous stories, painted, photographed, and recorded on celluloid. It has produced some of the world's most innovative musicians, talented chefs, best-selling authors, and infamous Lotharios—and every year it still throws one of the biggest parties on earth!

Founded by the French in the early 1700s, the city was part of a large tract of land that remained under European control until 1803. From its position on one of the most precipitous corners of the Mississippi River, the Crescent City (as it became known) controlled trade into the heartland of North America. Though it now proclaims its American credentials with certainty and pride, New Orleans (pronounced N'Awlins in the local accent) has never completely turned its back on European attitudes and values.

In the mid-18th century New Orleans was the focus of all activity in this very rich part of America. Here you had wealthy plantation owners, importers trading European goods, merchants and lawyers. They rubbed shoulders with sailors and itinerant workers in the bars, gaming houses, and brothels for which the city became renowned. Which other mix could have been responsible for the invention of craps, cocktails, and jazz?

Everything centers on the French Quarter, or Vieux Carré, the small square of streets first settled by the French and now the historical and spiritual heart of the city. The buildings date from the late 17th century, with stunning wrought-iron decoration, shady courtyards, plant-festooned balconies, and sheltered sidewalks. On Chartres and Royal Street you can almost imagine the Creole (those born in the colonies of European origin) ladies in their hooped crinoline dresses stepping out for a day of shopping for perfume from Paris or lace from Gentilly. Nearby Bourbon Street takes its cue from the more raucous episodes in New Orleans history. This is a place of excess, especially after night falls. You may not want to join in, but Bourbon Street holds a certain fascination, and the music clubs of the French Quarter are all within a stone's throw of each other. The musical talent is so strong here that even the buskers should have recording contracts.

Since the 1940s the French Quarter has been under a preservation order, which stemmed the encroachment of the worst of the 20th century. You'll find no high-rise buildings, billboards, or traffic lights here. From the moment you arrive you realize you're somewhere special. It's one of the destinations in the world where the atmosphere is palpable, almost as heady as the Louisiana air on long, hot, humid summer days. What makes the French Quarter special is that, although protected, it hasn't been packed in cotton wool. It's a place where real people live, with food stores, laundries, and cafés where people meet to discuss the latest news. Locals know their neighbors and strangers greet you in the street with a friendly smile and a "how y'all doin'?"

Of course New Orleans isn't just the French Quarter. By the early 18th century there were suburbs to the south, and in the mid-18th century large plantations to the north were broken up to create new towns later absorbed into the city. The city has lots of green spaces, parks, and trees; except for the compact high-rise Central Business District—a skyline visible for miles around—New Orleans is generally low-rise, with family homes, chairs on painted porches, and neatly lawned gardens accented by colorful potted plants.

Natives of New Orleans come from a variety of bloodlines. Some family names date back to the very birth of the city

—French settlers who helped develop the city became the Creole backbone of New Orleans history—and you'll see the same family names appearing again and again over the centuries, scribed on official documents or as the signatory on land deeds.

Almost immediately, the French were joined by numerous German families lured by the fraudulent sales pitch of John Law, who told them they were heading to a thriving city— in reality little more than a muddy field. Later came the Spanish, who ruled New Orleans in the late 1700s, followed by Italians and numerous Irish settlers fleeing the potato famine in

Lacy, wrought-iron balconies lend Royal Street a distinctive sophistication.

their homeland. Slaves were imported from Africa to work on the land, bringing little more with them than their distinctive cuisine, voodoo religious practices, and the throbbing beat of music played on skin drums. The Acadian French arrived in the mid-1800s, after being ejected from Canada. They found city life not to their liking and dispersed into the swamps and prairies to the west. Today the Cajuns, as they are known, still preserve a culture quite separate from the rest of the US.

The final settlers were Americans, following the Louisiana Purchase in 1803. Imagine their reaction when they arrived to find themselves strangers in their own country, where French was the first language and Paris was the focus, not New York. They were not welcomed by the Creoles and were forced to settle north of the French Quarter. Now known as the Garden District, this area is replete with architectural gems from the pretty clapboard cottages to the Greek columns on grand revival mansions.

Today, The Big Easy is, perhaps, the most permissive city in the US, an adult playground where it's OK to be a little naughty. You can drink all day and night—and in public—listen to music so loud that it would be considered a health hazard back home, and enjoy the delights of bare flesh, if that is your peccadillo. New Orleans still attracts a certain kind of person—artists, romantics, and people wanting to escape the restrictions of living someone else's

A horse and carriage offers visitors a tour through Bourbon Street in the French Quarter.

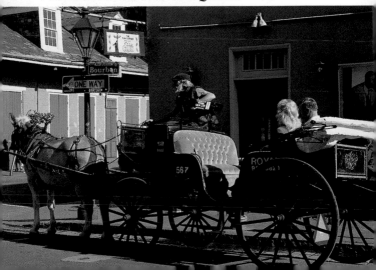

American dream. The city accommodates just about any lifestyle and has an established gay community along with a growing number of adherents to New Age philosophies. These people say that the city chooses them rather than the other way around; it just kind of gets under one's skin.

Native Crescent City dwellers also love their town. You'll meet them in the numerous excellent restaurants the city has to offer, at the theatre, or in jazz clubs in the early hours of the morning. On Sunday mornings the whole family heads to church dressed in their finest clothes — the population is predominantly Catholic, another legacy of French and Spanish rule — before enjoying a long brunch at a fine restaurant such as Commander's Palace or Brennan's. The social structures of over two centuries of settlement have created a closely-knit community, remarkably well integrated for a city in the southern states.

Perhaps more than most destinations, exploring the museums in New Orleans seems less important than simply being on the streets, listening to the music, and indulging your appetites. Just sitting over strong coffee and sweet beignets is very New Orleans. It's OK to throw away your pre-planned itinerary and indulge in the luxury of not doing anything at all.

At any time of year, a trip to the Big Easy can be like one long party, but the granddaddy of all celebrations is Mardi Gras, or Fat Tuesday, when the city bids "farewell to the flesh" before starting its Lenten fast. It says a lot about New Orleans that, at its heart, this huge series of parades, parties, and *soirées* is really a local carnival organized by local people. If the rest of the world wants to join in that's fine, but if outsiders decide not to accept the invitation, the party will simply happen without them. This is not an event just laid out for and sustained by tourists.

The New Orleans skyline at dusk shows off a modern city which is at once cosmopolitan and offbeat.

The fact that this is a city where people are still making history, and not simply living with its effects, is what makes New Orleans such an enjoyable place to be. The music scene is as vibrant as it has always been, with a world-renowned jazz festival taking place each year, and the city is at the forefront of a culinary revolution which has New Orleans chefs and their signature dishes achieving world-wide recognition.

In many ways New Orleans defies description. At every turn there is something to see, hear, taste, and touch; things that will amaze you, maybe even shock you a bit. The best way to deal with this is to grab a cocktail and throw yourself into the party—there's really no other place like New Orleans for that!

A BRIEF HISTORY

It seems like a rather strange site for a colonial city. The Mississippi was untamed when the location was found by the French and changed course regularly through the vast flat delta its power had created. The site is below sea level (even below river level), hot and sticky in the long summer, surrounded by pestilential swamps, vulnerable to every flood and hurricane, and more than 100 miles (160 km) from the Gulf of Mexico—or anywhere else. How did it hope to compete with the great coastal settlements in other parts of the New World?

The Native Americans (Choctaws and other tribes) who settled here thousands of years before the arrival of the French colonists lived a simple life. Although they needed to avoid water snakes, alligators, and disease-carrying mosquitoes, they enjoyed a cornucopia of seafood and game, flavoring it with a hot sauce the Creoles would later adopt. They used the waterways of the Mississippi delta as highways, navigating their dugout canoes through the impenetrable and ever-changing maze of bayous.

The first European to see the Mississippi was the Spanish Conquistador Hernando de Soto, brother-in-law of Balboa and the discoverer of the Pacific. The French connection was to begin in 1682 when René Robert Cavelier, Sieur de La Salle, claimed for France a huge swath of territory radiating from the Mississippi. In honor of his king, Louis XIV, he gave it the name *Louisiane.*

Seventeen years later, France sent a further expedition, led by Pierre le Moyne, Sieur d'Iberville. Along with his younger brother, Jean-Baptiste, Sieur de Bienville, he established several tentative settlements along the Mississippi. In 1718 Bienville marked the spot for New Orleans. The brothers are remembered today as the true founders of both the state and

the city—Bienville later served as the first governor of
Louisiana. Interestingly, they were Creole French—off-
spring of French nationals born in Montreal.

Hanky-Panky by Law

Meanwhile, a European with an eye for chance had ingrati-
ated his way into the French court at Versailles. John Law, a
Scotsman, financier, and high-rolling gambler, on the run
from England after a fatal duel, saw the possibility of pro-
moting this distant marshland as a paradise. Luckily for New
Orleans, his scheme was a remarkable success.

Law brokered a deal with the French government, giving
him a 25-year charter to develop the Louisiana Territory. All
he needed were investors and settlers, whom he lured with a
campaign of propaganda. On posters Law distributed in
France, New Orleans was pictured as a prosperous seaport.
When Law's clients arrived after months at sea, the truth of
the Mississippi Bubble was plain. The only housing available was huts or tents, and the roads were generally quag-
mires. But there was nowhere else to go, so the pioneers
were forced to pitch in and try to survive.

John Law's promotional activities weren't confined to the
French. He signed up some 10,000 Germans, mostly Rhine-
landers, to share the "golden future" in Louisiana. Today,
west of New Orleans along what is called the German Coast,
you can see towns with names like Hahnville, Kraemer, and
Des Allemands. Most descendants of the German pioneers,
however, Frenchified their names, thus Delmaire was originally Edelmeyer and Fauquel was Vogel.

Black slaves from Africa also arrived in the earliest years
of the colony. In 1724, the Bienville enacted the *Code Noir*
(Black Code), which regulated the conditions of slavery and
the rights of free blacks. The code, more liberal than the laws

Historic Dixieland—The Creole Queen paddle steamer, with Chalmette battlefield in the background.

elsewhere in the South, remained in force in Louisiana for a century. As for the Mississippi Bubble, it burst in 1720. France came out of the deal bankrupt and with huge pieces of land considered to be worthless. John Law died in 1729, dispossessed in Venice.

High Society

By the middle of the 18th century, New Orleans had grown into a town—not exactly self-sufficient, but beyond the survival stage. To carry this a step farther, the Marquis de Vaudreuil, Governor Bienville's successor in 1743, attempted to transform New Orleans into an overseas Versailles. *A bon vivant* who held extravagant parties, Vaudreuil and his elegant wife presided over a sort of "Golden Age" of social grace, when the colonial elite were invited to plays, musicales, and balls. His serious

The golden statue of Jean D'Arc symbolizes New Orleans' French roots.

business included organizing the first system of man-made levees to protect the city from the Mississippi. At the same time, the governor and his cronies were busily pocketing bribes, as was the custom in the self-financing French colonial service. He can therefore be considered as the founder of a grand old Louisiana tradition—political corruption.

¡Caramba!

The Treaty of Fontainebleau in 1762 brought a shattering blow to the population of Louisiana. Overnight, it appeared, they had been handed over to King Charles III of Spain—though the treaty was not announced until 1764. It all made perfect sense to King Louis XV, cousin of Charles (both were Bourbons), for the French and Indian War, known in Europe as the Seven Years War, had been disastrous for French interests abroad. Britain won Canada and everything east of the Mississippi, including Spanish Florida. To Louis, Louisiana was now isolated in a British-ruled part of the world, a money-losing outpost that seemed to have no future.

It must have come as an almost unbearable shock to the patriotic Frenchmen of New Orleans to be told that they were Spanish citizens. Waiting for the first Spanish governor to arrive put a huge strain on the disillusioned society. When Governor Antonio de Ulloa finally sailed up the Mississippi in 1766, four years after the treaty was signed, a crashing storm erupted, as if an omen for the climate ahead. The governor, a scholarly retired naval officer with good intentions, was accompanied by a contingent of 80 Spanish soldiers, most of retirement age.

The high-society frolics of the Vaudreuil era were over; the Spanish governor's wife froze out the Creole ladies of New Orleans from official invitation lists. French-speaking citizens protested the snub with a petition and a demonstration that got out of control and turned into violence. Spain called it treason. The harassed Ulloa could take no more and sailed into exile.

The second governor sent from Spain, Lieutenant General Don Alejandro O'Reilly, cracked down on the rebels. O'Reilly created the Cabildo, or town council, and led New Orleans toward prosperity. But he is remembered with bitterness. To assert Spain's authority and extinguish dissent, he ordered the execution of five Creole rebels. They stood before the firing squad on the Esplanade near where it crosses Frenchmen Street, named in their memory.

The Acadians

During the troubled Spanish era, thousands of French exiles from eastern Canada—Acadians, shortened to Cajuns— migrated to Louisiana. For years their territory had been the target of a struggle between the British and French, and the emphatic British victory in the French and Indian War forced them to leave, when they refused to swear allegiance to the British Crown.

The hubbub of New Orleans was too much for them and they settled into the surrounding countryside. Unlike the other colonists, who eventually melted into the culture, the Cajuns kept to themselves in the bayou, retaining their 17th-century language and customs. Only in the 20th century did they start to communicate in English as well. The present Cajun population in Louisiana, numbering in the hundreds of thousands, is still largely parochial. But one aspect of their culture, their spicy cuisine, has become fashionable across the United States and, more recently, the world.

The French Quarter

In 1788 a Spanish official, lighting a devotional candle in the private chapel in his home on Chartres Street, started a fire which spread, fanned by the wind, to devour nearly half the town. In 1794 another blaze swept through the streets. New Orleans looked on the positive side of these disasters. Taking note of the obvious vulnerability of the old wooden houses, the government set up new building standards. Tile roofs became the rule, and structures with more than a single floor had to be built of brick. Spanish-colonial touches such as garden patios, shaded balconies, and adornments of wrought iron gave the area its almost Caribbean air. This new town became known, ironically, as the French Quarter or Vieux Carré.

Revolutionary Antics

During the American Revolution, New Orleans plunged in on the revolutionist side. It wasn't only enthusiasm for the Yankees; Spain declared war on England in 1779. The governor of New Orleans, 23-year-old Don Bernardo de Gálvez, seized the chance to help the colonists in their struggle against George III, and led raiding parties that kept the British outposts along the Mississippi on the defensive.

After the American Revolution came the French Revolution and a new world order. The ambitions of Napoléon

Bonaparte stretched as far as the Western Hemisphere, and an influx of French aristocrats buoyed French sentiments. By the secret Treaty of Ildefonso in 1800, France regained Louisiana from Spain after 38 years.

But in 1803, only three years after retaking it, France sold Louisiana to the United States for $15 million. It was a controversial amount at the time—more than the US Treasury owned—but the Louisiana Purchase, as it became known, covered land from Canada to the Rockies to the Gulf of Mexico, and almost doubled the area of the United States. The deal turned out to be the bargain of all time—something like four cents an acre for what became Iowa, Arkansas, Missouri, Nebraska, South Dakota, and most of Kansas, Louisiana, and Oklahoma.

As usual, New Orleans was among the last to learn this, thanks to the secrecy of diplomatic negotiations and the slow communications of the age. In the event, within one month three different flags flew over the *Place d'Armes* (now Jackson Square). The Stars and Stripes replaced the French flag on 20 December 1803, only three weeks after the Spanish gave way to the French. Once again, the stunned citizens felt abandoned and betrayed.

The Yanks Are Coming!

President Jefferson's choice of governor for the Territory of Orleans seemed, to say the least, inauspicious. William Charles Cole Claiborne was a Protestant from Virginia who needed interpreters to communicate in both French and Spanish. He judged the Creoles honest but lazy and ill-educated, their town ugly and filthy—though his horror at the city's sanitation was understandable; he would lose two wives to yellow fever in New Orleans. In return, the local Creoles considered themselves "more worldly" than the rustic

Americans. Claiborne persevered, however, learned French, changed the laws, and brought his carping constituents into the American fold as citizens of the new State of Louisiana, even though it was very much unlike any other US state.

War on the Mississippi

Less than two months after Louisiana won its statehood, the United States went to war with Britain—for the second and last time. To everyone's surprise, New Orleans became the stage for the most glorious, indeed the only, American victory of the whole conflict.

The War of 1812 was fostered by accumulated American grievances. There were dramatic naval battles and a final ghastly defeat for the United States when the British burned down the city of Washington. Finally, the warring parties focused on New Orleans. A British flotilla, diverted from the Caribbean, sailed up the Mississippi with some 10,000 first-class troops. The Americans rushed Major General Andrew Jackson to New Orleans to command the city's defense. Outmanned and outgunned, Jackson mobilized a force of somewhat irregular members: an unlikely coalition of militiamen, local Creoles, free blacks, Choctaws, and associates of the privateers Jean and Pierre Lafitte (see page 74). The pirates may well have been the key to the outcome, for they alone knew the ins and outs of the bayou country, from where the British attack would come.

In the Battle of Orleans—fought in Chalmette down the river—General Sir Edward Packenham and his redcoats marched in proper formation across the battlefield like toy soldiers—straight into the American artillery. In less than half an hour it was all over: General Packenham, the brother-in-law of the Duke of Wellington (famous for his war successes), had been shot, thousands of his troops had been killed, and the tattered survivors withdrew in disarray. Ironically, the war was already over. A peace treaty had been signed in Belgium two weeks before, but news traveled no faster than a ship in those days.

Between Wars

By the 1830s, New Orleans had reached its heyday. The sound of post-war prosperity was the blast of steam whistles on the river. With the development of powerful steamboats, navigation on the Mississippi became a practical, economical matter. Freighters moved cotton, tobacco, and sugar downriver and worldwide. Passenger ships like the *Natchez* and the *Belle of Memphis* were palaces with food, drink, music, and romance, at a time when even short journeys could take many days.

Oak Alley plantation is named for the lovely tree-lined driveway leading to the main house.

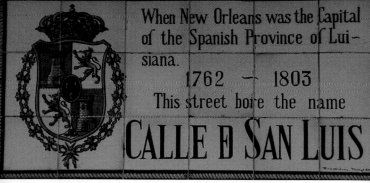

When New Orleans was the Capital of the Spanish Province of Luisiana.
1762 — 1803
This street bore the name
CALLE D SAN LUIS

A tiled street sign in the French Quarter illustrates a legacy of Spanish power in the Crescent City.

Thousands of steamboats docked along the quays every year. By 1840 New Orleans was the world's largest cotton port, second only to New York as a general port, and the fourth biggest city in the United States, with a population of 100,000. American families, who came south looking for a place to settle, found themselves unwelcome in the French Quarter. Instead they created a second city upriver—now the Garden District— using the plentiful land that once constituted sugar plantations.

It was also the era of benefactors both in social and cultural fields. One was John McDonogh, who elevated conditions for the ordinary people of the city. A plantation owner of Scottish extraction, he educated and freed many slaves. Most of City Park is land he willed to the children of New Orleans. When he died, a millionaire, in 1850 (back when a million dollars really meant something), he left his money to the city to build schools for the poor. Dozens are still named after McDonogh, who, in effect, founded the city's public school system.

At this time less than half of the black population were slaves, and those that were led a less onerous life than in most other parts of the South. "Free people of color" ran their own businesses and owned property. Free women of color were included among the concubines of white aristocrats, their lives organized according to arcane social codes.

Culture thrived in this climate. Carnival parades began in 1837, although other aspects of Mardi Gras festivities had taken hold much earlier. The French Opera House, at the corner of Bourbon and Toulouse streets, opened in 1859 and supported the nation's first resident opera company. On quite another cultural plane, a 1798 law against gambling was ignored in New Orleans, where the card game of poker is said to have originated. The merchant seaman, plantation owners, and businessmen who thronged the city streets also looked for the distraction of other pleasures, and prostitution was rife in the less salubrious parts of town.

The War between the States

In January 1861, Louisiana joined other cotton states in seceding from Lincoln's Union. After two months as an independent entity, the state entered the new Confederacy, but because of its strategic significance, New Orleans became a high-priority target for the northern military forces.

In April 1862, a Union naval force led by David G. Farragut capitalized on Confederate unpreparedness and penetrated the defenses of New Orleans. Despite localized opposition, within a week, the Union flag was raised over the city. It announced a military occupation destined to endure beyond the Civil War (or War between the States, as it is known in the south) into the Reconstruction period—for a total of 14 bitter years. The reconstruction of New Orleans began in 1879, when the jetties were built to speed the flow of the Mississippi near its mouth. This improved navigation and returned the port to a position of strength. New railway lines linked the city with the rest of the United States.

In 1884 the city attempted to demonstrate its post-war recovery by staging an international fair—the World's Industrial and Cotton Centennial Exposition—on the site of what is now Audubon Park. The morale-boosting exercise lost money, but the rest of the United States had started to hear about the industrious but amusing city on the Mississippi as a place worth visiting.

The Storyville Story

In 1897, in an attempt to curb the worst excesses of the Big Easy, Alderman Sidney Story created a city ordinance outlawing prostitution everywhere in the city except for a small, specific area just beyond the French Quarter, where it could be contained and controlled. This area, known as Storyville, became a leg-

---

Sons and Daughters of New Orleans

The hotbed of influences that is New Orleans has produced many famous and interesting sons and daughters. They include:

Louis Armstrong–world famous jazz musician
John Hampson–inventor of Venetian blinds
George Herriman–cartoonist
William Jefferson–first African-American since Reconstruction to be elected to Congress
Dorothy Lamour–actress
Marie Laveau–Voodoo Queen
Josef Delarose Lascaux–inventor of cotton candy
Paul Morphy–world chess champion at 21
Anne Rice–author
Richard Simmons–exercise and nutrition guru

---

end in its own time, where the mixture of glamour, depravity, and color in the local brothels attracted almost every visiting celebrity, and where saloon drinkers, gamblers, and rakes waiting their turn could tap their feet to a developing style of music — jazz. Louis Armstrong started playing his bent, nickel-plated cornet in the dives of Storyville. He improvised from evening to daybreak for 15 cents a night.

Storyville lasted exactly 20 years. In World War I the US Navy Department ordered the creation of a vice-free zone for five miles around every naval base. That included Storyville, and the place closed down.

Houses for the dead: tombs of the rich and famous at Lafayette Cemetery.

The Long Saga

In Louisiana, politics and politicians have always been a fascinating business — and business is the word — but none of the bosses could compare with larger-than life Huey P. Long (1893–1935). Long was cagey, ambitious, poor, and so bright he graduated from Tulane Law School less than a year after he entered. At the age of 25 he was elected to the state public service commission; as governor he built roads and bridges that were desperately needed, and supplied all the state's school children with free textbooks. His slogans were "Every Man a King" and "A Chicken in Every Pot."

Elected to the US Senate, he still controlled Louisiana from Washington, having installed a puppet in the governor's office. Long was starting to attract a national following when he was assassinated in the state capitol in Baton Rouge on 8 September 1935.

During the latter years of Long's reign, the French Quarter had reached a nadir, with many fine buildings in a state of near collapse — some were even demolished to make parking lots. In 1936, the state set up the Vieux Carré Commission with powers to protect buildings of architectural value. It still operates to control development in the area.

Baton Rouge is a major port and industrial center, as well as being the home of the state government.

Meanwhile oil had been discovered in Louisiana in 1901. The land was transformed by hundreds of small wells sunk to extract the precious liquid. In 1947 the first offshore rig was opened and the Mississippi valley became a hub of oil and gas production and storage. After the Second World War new highways led to broader horizons, and suburbs began to sprawl. Following the construction of the impressive causeway across Lake Pontchartrain in 1956, commuters even began to move to the far side of the lake, and NASA assembled thousands of technicians at suburban Michoud to produce its booster rockets.

Desegregation in schools, which hit many southern cities hard in the 1960s, passed off in New Orleans with a minimum of trouble. Whites and blacks had always mixed more freely here than in most places in Dixie, and the drive for racial equality reached an historic high in 1977 when Judge Ernest "Dutch" Morial was elected the first African-American mayor.

Today "Dutch's" son Marc carries on the family tradition as Mayor. But if the city seems to be moving in a positive direction, the state has other problems. As the third millennium begins, Louisiana is again suffering the problem that has plagued it throughout its history. Federal racketeering charges have been brought against Edwin Edwards—Louisiana State Governor until his retirement in 1996—and the huge trial in Baton Rouge is keeping the state on the edge of its seat. It seems that little has changed since the times of John Law.

New Orleans seems to move from strength to strength. In recent years new cultural and recreational facilities have multiplied the city's tourist potential. These include greatly expanded riverfront parks, a state-of-the-art aquarium, and a revived warehouse district.

WHERE TO GO

New Orleans is unique in America. Because of the bends in the Mississippi, the normal north, south, east, and west directions cannot apply without great confusion. Local people will always give you directions upriver, downriver, lakeside (toward lake Pontchartrain), or riverside (toward the river). The French Quarter is always seen as the center of New Orleans, so generally the terms above will refer to directions from here.

The French Quarter is relatively simple to explore—a simple, compact grid of streets, there are many street signs and the city limits are bounded by easily identified, wide thoroughfares. Upriver from the French Quarter you will find the Central Business District (CBD), the Warehouse District, the Garden District, and the University area. Downriver is the suburb of Faubourg Marigny, leading to Chalmette, where the Battle of New Orleans was fought. Lakeside are more modern suburbs which include in their bounds City Park and the Jazz Fest grounds.

We'll begin by exploring the French Quarter, but before you start on foot, one of the best ways to get your bearings would be to take a carriage ride through the streets. Your driver will offer a wealth of information about the Quarter, and you'll be able to get above the crowds for a better view.

☛ THE FRENCH QUARTER

The French Quarter was once all there was of New Orleans. In French it is called the Vieux Carré, and you will still see references to this name throughout your stay. A tightly packed square of 13 blocks, it was surrounded by swamps dotted with large plantations. The city was a point of contact with the rest of the world for the Louisiana population, with silks and perfumes from Paris for the ladies, the latest news on market prices for their husbands. When the French Quarter suffered two devastating fires in the late 1700s, the Spanish colonial overlords rebuilt the city along the same lines but in brick—and for the most part this is what we see today. The streets are lined with fine mansions; some are still family homes, others have been put to a variety of commercial uses. Many are decorated with beautiful wrought ironwork. You'll see pretty, cool courtyards behind the façades. Delightful Creole cottages line the streets on the outer

The charm of the French Quarter is based in its regal architecture.

fringes—their gingerbread trim kept spick and span by regular coats of paint.

The best way to take in all this splendor is to simply stroll around. Take your time to read every bronze plaque (these have been affixed to the major important structures and give points of interest such as the date of construction and the like), and note every little detail.

Of course the French Quarter isn't just about the pretty views. The famed atmosphere of the place is palpable—music can be heard on every street corner, dancing youngsters vie for your dollars, and street performers pose for your photos. The aromas of a hundred restaurants drift tantalizingly in the air and shop windows beckon with beautiful displays. Your senses are sure to be seduced at every turn, so be prepared!

Whether you tour on foot or by carriage, the starting place is **Jackson Square**—the focal point of the Quarter that almost sits at the riverside. Originally named the Place des Armes by the French because it was drilling ground for their troops, it was renamed after General Andrew Jackson in 1848 following his stoic defense of the city in the Battle of New Orleans. There is a statue of the general at the heart of the park filling the center of the square—a good place to rest, or plan your tour.

Wide cobbled walkways surround the park, and the buildings lining Jackson Square reflect its importance to the city. **St. Louis Cathedral** is the oldest cathedral in the US, having been inaugurated in 1794—though parish churches had stood on the site from 1718. The present structure dates from 1849.

Flanking the Cathedral are two identical buildings, each built for a different purpose. To the left, the **Cabildo** (its name is derived from the governing body of the city) was built between 1795–1799 to house the Spanish colonial government, whose representatives had just taken power. As the

Dixieland

All of the southern United States is known as Dixie, or Dixieland, thanks to a lively song by Dan Emmett. In 1861 the tune emerged from minstrel shows to become the unofficial anthem of the Confederacy. The origin of the name, though, can be traced to New Orleans. In 1860 the Citizens' Bank of Louisiana issued $10 bills with "TEN" printed on one side and the French equivalent, "DIX," on the other. New Orleans was soon called "Dixie," and the label was eventually applied to the whole South.

city's longest standing official building, its walls have seen many historical events. It is now a part of the Louisiana State Museum Complex. An excellent introduction to the history of the diverse state that is modern Louisiana, the museum takes visitors from the first exploration of the bayous by the Bienville brothers to the signing of the Louisiana Purchase, which took place in an upper chamber here in 1803. The antebellum lifestyle of the Creoles is explained, as are the devastating effects of the Civil War on the region. Napoleon's death mask, given to the city by his doctor, occupies a place of honor at the top of the main staircase. Finally, the changes to the modern city in the era of film and photography can be studied. Behind the Cabildo, yet attached to it, is the **old Arsenal** (1825), though this building is not the original. Long-term temporary exhibitions are shown here—enter through the museum.

To the right of the Cathedral is the **Presbytère**, which sits on the site of an old Capuchin monastery destroyed in the 1788 fire. This building was conceived as a place of residence for the clergy under Spanish rule, but was actually completed after the Louisiana Purchase in 1803 and never used for religious purposes. It now houses another division of

St. Louis Cathedral presides over a horse and carriage in Jackson Square.

The Mardi Gras exhibit in the Presbytère displays all the strangeness and splendor of the actual event.

the museum complex, focusing on Mardi Gras. **The Mardi Gras Museum** will fill in background details about the history of the "krewe" system, and reveals some of the colorful characters who have graced carnival floats over the preceding years. The costumed displays look great, but it is the video footage of parades that really brings home the surreal experience that is Mardi Gras; if you can't make it to New Orleans during the festival time, this museum is the next best way to experience it.

The other flanks of Jackson Square are lined with colonnaded buildings housing stores at ground level. Construction of these was funded in the 1840s by the Baroness de Pontalba, one of the richest women in Spanish New Orleans, to both improve the Place des Armes and provide up-market residences for the population. Many of the apartments in the **Pontalba**

Buildings are still residential, though the structures are national monuments. At 525 St. Ann Street you will be able to explore the **1850 House**, restored as a typical dwelling of the time. You will also find the **New Orleans Welcome Center** on St. Ann (on the downriver side), where you will be able to obtain maps and other information to plan your itinerary.

From Jackson Square, the heart of the French Quarter sits away from the river. It comprises a series of straight interlinking streets, easy to explore on foot because traffic moves slowly or is nonexistent; many areas are pedestrian-only during the day. This guide will explore the major attractions on each major street running parallel to the river—that is Chartres, Royal, and Bourbon—and working outward.

> Forget about using an automobile—enjoy strolling.

Chartres Street (pronounced Charters) intersects Jackson Square in front of the Cathedral. At this corner is **Le Petit Théâtre du Vieux Carré**, the oldest continually operating community theatre in the US. The company was founded in 1919 and still holds regular performances. Heading upriver to the corner of St. Louis, the **New Orleans Pharmacy Museum** sits at the site of the first registered apothecary shop in the country, which opened in 1823. Many potions and medicines were manufactured in-house at this time, but this shop also produced perfumes and voodoo remedies. Apothecary paraphernalia is displayed here, including bottles, scales, and weights, along with an interesting exhibit examining "milestones in the history of pharmacy and medicine."

Chartres boasts one of the oldest buildings in the city at its downriver end (turn right as you face the Cathedral), the **Old Ursuline Convent**, at number 1114. The Sisters of St. Ursula moved into the building in 1749; from here they controlled schooling for the region, particularly for the poor and powerless, including city orphans. When the sisters moved to another site in 1824, the building stood vacant for a few years, and was then used to house the State Legislature from 1830–1834.

Directly across the street from the convent is the **Beauregard-Keyes House** (also called the LeCarpentier House). Joseph LeCarpentier bought a large amount of land from the nuns, erecting this house on one of the lots in 1827. In 1866, General P. G. T. Beauregard (who ordered the attack on Fort Sumpter that kicked off the Civil War) rented a room here, and more recently the house was home to the authoress Francis Parkinson Keyes— hence the convoluted name. From the house, take a left and then a left again down Governor Nicholls, where you will find **Soniat House**, constructed in 1829 and decorated with remarkable wrought ironwork.

> No matter where your wanderings take you, always be prepared for an afternoon rainstorm.

The next thoroughfare is **Royal Street**, or Rue Royale, with its wealth of architectural detail—perhaps the most photographed street in New Orleans. On the corner of Royal and Governor Nicholls is **LaLaurie House**, at number 1140, said to be haunted by the ghosts of slaves badly treated by their mistress, Delphine LaLaurie. **Gallier House** (1857) stands at 1132. James Gallier Junior, a prominent architect, designed this home for himself and his family. Recent renovations have thoroughly restored the place to accurately portray its appearance and furnishings during the Galliers' time here. Carry on strolling along Royal Street, toward the distant skyscrapers of the Central Business District and past a few blocks of stores and tiny galleries. On the right is the **Cornstalk Hotel**, named after its famous fence; the elaborate row of stalks of corn fashioned from wrought iron was erected in 1834. The hotel was built as a private house in classic Victorian style around 1850.

Just beyond the hotel, you will reach Dumaine Street; take a left. A little way along, at number 623, stands **Madame John's Legacy**, a French-Colonial–style home that some experts argue is actually the oldest in New Orleans. Documents prove that the present structure was built just after the fire of 1788—on the site of another house which dated from the 1720s and was owned by Manuel de Lanzos. Since his death in 1729, the house has seen more than 20 owners. It is now the property of the Louisiana State Museum, which has restored its rare brick-and-post construction. Its strange name derives from a George W. Cable short story, in which it was bequeathed to the fictional lead character. At 724 Dumaine is the **New Orleans**

Both writers and generals have graced the stately rooms of the Beauregard-Keyes House.

Musicians entertain the diners at the Court of Two Sisters restaurant.

Historic Voodoo Museum, a privately run museum offering an interesting introduction to this secretive and misunderstood form of worship. You won't uncover the inner secrets of voodoo here, but you will learn the basic principles. There are displays of amulets and other occult objects to view, and the proprietors practice voodoo, so you can ask questions, get a reading, and buy a genuine *gris-gris* bag for good luck (gris is the French word for grey, and indicates a magic somewhere between black and white).

Return to Royal Street and continue to stroll in the same direction as before. The architecture grows more beautiful, and the galleries and antique shops become larger and more exquisite as you travel. Most of the buildings in this part of the Quarter have a long history to tell—look for details such as Spanish street signs or ornate tiles as evidence of the past. Official bronze plaques offer useful information about each structure. Number 613 now houses the **Court of Two Sisters restaurant**—which has a pretty inner courtyard. Dating from the early 1800s, the building was owned by the Camors sisters, who for many years operated an upscale ladies' emporium. They began to provide food for their customers, who often traveled great dis-

Whatever your opinion, it is not to be missed: The bars are filled with great music, and you can stroll down the street with a "cocktail to go," be invited into nude bars, and watch people do just about anything for a string of carnival beads. Street entertainers are plentiful here, so make sure you have some small change.

Roughly speaking, the tackiest end of Bourbon is upriver (toward Canal Street), though you may be surprised to find fine restaurants standing side-by-side with less salubrious neighbors. Downriver from here is an area predominated by bars and restaurants—those with balconies being the most popular. Scattered all along Bourbon are souvenir stores selling T-shirts with questionable slogans, beads by the pound, masks, and other fun stuff. At the intersection of Bienville, look to your left at the entrance to **Arnaud's Restaurant**— one of the finest in the city. "Count" Arnaud Cazanave founded it in 1918; his family was at the forefront of the New Orleans social scene. The Count's daughter Germaine was Queen of more Mardi Gras balls then any other women in history, during a reign lasting from 1937 to 1968. Above the restaurant is a museum dedicated to Germaine, including many of her costumes and photographs of the family at various Mardi Gras celebrations, bringing the costumes to life.

When you reach Conti, take a short detour to number 917, the **Museé Conti Wax Museum**. This museum features a number of dioramas depicting important people and events in Louisiana's history. When the air-conditioning ruffles the clothing on the models, you will be forgiven for thinking that they have come to life. Adults will enjoy the Chamber of Horrors, which includes all the favorites from the werewolf to *The Pit and the Pendulum*. Once back outside, make a left at St. Louis to find **Hermann-Grima House**. Built in 1831,

Experience grandeur in the style of the 19th century southern aristocracy at the Hermann-Grima House.

this is a handsome mansion with a courtyard, the only house to have a working outdoor kitchen. The beautifully furnished rooms evoke the lifestyle of a wealthy prominent family of the time.

Back on Bourbon, at the corner of Peter Street is Maison de Flechier, which is now occupied by **Pat O'Brien's Bar**—famous for the Hurricane cocktail. Enjoy the beautiful courtyard while you take some refreshment. Turn down St. Peter Street to find **Preservation Hall** on the right. Since the 1960s, this old stable building has worked to preserve the true tradition of jazz. No food or drink is allowed in the hall and no tickets are sold; you simply wait in line at the door and drop your money in a collection bowl. The music played inside is the pure essence of the art of syncopation. Farther down Bourbon is **Lafitte's Blacksmith Shop**—yes, yet another bar, but with a different atmosphere from its loud and raunchy neighbors. Set in a building dating from the late 1700s, legend says that the smithy was owned and operated by the famous Lafitte brothers, though no definite proof of this exists.

THE WATERFRONT

The Mississippi is the *raison d'être* for the city and still important to its modern-day prosperity, as New Orleans sits at the heart of one of the largest ports in the world. The river is wide and deep at its passage through the city, but the amount of silt it carries makes it a dull brown color—perhaps a little disappointing, but no less fascinating. Of course the fact that New Orleans was a trading town always dictated the riverfront development. It was never going to be pretty when it had to be functional; consequently, basic warehouses lined the banks until just recently, and rail tracks used to transport freight bisect the short walk from Jackson Square to the river. Today, the main wharves lie outside the downtown area and the waterfront has undergone something of a revival. Several major attractions can be found within a few feet of the water.

On the river side of Jackson Square is **Washington Artillery**. This small, raised site with its shiny black cannon is a great place for photographs, offering wonderful views of Jackson Square and the Cathedral. Washington Artillery is divided from Jackson Square by **Decatur Street**. Strictly speaking this street is the southern boundary of the French Quarter.

From Washington Artillery you can either head upriver or downriver. It is possible to stroll for perhaps 20 minutes on a walkway—called Moonwalk by the locals—beside the water. If you are tired of walking, the Riverfront streetcar runs along the same path; at $1.25 per journey, the ride may help you regain your breath while allowing you to take in the sights.

There is little to see at the water's edge downriver from Washington Artillery. Instead, head down Decatur Street, where you will find **French Market** on the left. This large complex was the site of Indian trading in the early history of New Orleans. The Spanish built many of the present buildings, creating a market area for the city. Today French Market is a fascinating blend of food, collectibles, souvenirs, and eateries; it's a really great place for browsing. The market occupies several buildings; the one closest to Washington Artillery is home to **Café du Monde**, a New Orleans institution, where everyone meets for *café au lait* and *beignets*.

Walking through the market you'll pass a beautiful shiny gold **statue of Joan of Arc** sitting astride a noble steed. Behind Joan is the **Farmers' Market**, stocked with fresh and dried chilies, plus tomatoes and fruit. The **Flea Market**, a veritable treasure-trove of collectibles and souvenir bargains, stands at the very far end.

Behind the lines of market stalls you will be able to make

The French Market brings home the novelty and variety of New Orleans.

out the imposing lines of a large grey building which looks like a fortress without protective walls. This is the **Old US Mint**, which produced coinage for the government from 1838–1861 and 1879–1910. It also produced Confederate coins in the early years— before Confederate

> Always carry lots of change and small bills to give to street performers and musicians.

gold supplies became exhausted. The first floor of the building now serves as a museum of the mint, and there is an interesting gift shop selling a selection of gold coins and dollar notes. The second floor is given over completely to **The New Orleans Jazz Exhibition** (known locally as The Jazz Museum). Over 20,000 objects relating to the development of this musical genre and its greatest exponents can be found here, including a cornet owned by Louis Armstrong and a piano belonging to Bix Beiderbecke. All the displays are organized in chronological order, which fosters an understanding of the timeline of jazz. There are numerous photographs that bring the individuals to life, and you'll hear jazz music from each era as you study the displays.

Upriver, **Woldenberg Park** sits on the riverbank, with a raised walkway above the water. This is a great place to come for an alfresco lunch, or just to sit and watch the world go by. The Woldenberg bandstand may host live musicians, but if not you will often hear impromptu performances from passing buskers. The steamer *Natchez*, the only steam-powered ship left in New Orleans, is berthed here. If you arrive around 11am you will hear its calliope (steam-powered organ) playing Dixieland tunes, heralding the boarding time for another journey. Across the rail tracks are the old **Jackson Brewery** buildings (locally known as the Jax), dating from the early 20th century and now converted into a shopping mall.

At the upriver end of Woldenberg Park, the cityscape begins to change and more modern architecture breaks the skyline. Two large bridges cross the river just ahead: called the Crescent City Connection, they carry rail and road traffic to the western suburbs. On the left is one of the most distinctive buildings in the city, the **Aquarium of the Americas**—part of the Audubon Institute—with a wealth of sea life to enjoy. The exhibits are divided into various aquatic environments, from the local Mississippi River and Gulf of Mexico to the Amazon and Caribbean. A recently arrived pair of sea otters have stolen everyone's hearts with their playful antics. Next door to the Aquarium is the Entergy **IMAX Cinema**, showing regular features about the natural world on its 3-D, 5-story-high screen. The Audubon Institute also operates the Zoological Gardens (see page 59) and a small ferry service between the two sites runs four times a day; it is possible to buy combined tickets.

The Aquarium of the Americas houses thousands of beautiful aquatic creatures.

Just beyond the Aquarium is the docking point for the **Canal Street Ferry**, which carries people and vehicles across the river to the settlement of Algiers. The ferry is free to foot passengers, so take the 5-minute journey across, even if it is only to gaze back at the New Orleans skyline and snap a few pictures.

The settlement of Algiers is a real contrast to its bigger cousin across the water. It has a small-town atmosphere, feeling perhaps a little left behind in time—its major period of development happened after the Civil War. At the ferry stop, you'll find small mini-buses that will transport you to **Blaine Kern's Mardi Gras World** just a couple of minutes away. Blaine Kern's produces figures and floats in fiberglass and papier mâché for many clients, including Disneyland, and for films, but the bulk of its work is to create the floats for all the major Mardi Gras parades. The company works in close partnership with the various krewes to produce bespoke float designs, and to redevelop old floats for new

Along the River

There are several boat tours that will carry you down the Mississippi on a two- or three-hour cruise. The view from the water makes clear how low-lying the French Quarter is (you'll see the infamous levees, built to contain any rise in water level), and how important trade has always been to her continued development. There are 21 miles (34 km) of warehouses and wharves on both sides of the city.

There's little history left along the waterfront, but some tours take in the battlefield at Chalmette, where the American beat the British in the Battle of New Orleans. The steam-boat *Natchez*, 265 ft (87 m) in length, doesn't stop at the battlefield, but the smaller Creole Queen operates a cruise which allows passengers to alight at Chalmette and spend an hour exploring the **Chalmette National Historic Park**, including the military cemetery and **Beauregard House** dating from 1833.

parades. Visitors can tour the vast warehouses, watching the work as it happens, and really getting close to the huge, ornate structures.

Bear in mind as you travel back across the water that **Algiers Point**, just off to your right, is one of the most acute bends in the river, requiring great care and expertise to navigate. The river is over 200 ft (63 m) deep here, which indicates just how much water flows past the city each day.

The ferry dock site on the city side sits at the foot of a huge skyscraper, the **World Trade Center**. Although much of the building is given over to office space, you can take the lift up to the 31st floor for magnificent views of the city. The **Top of the Mart** is a cocktail bar whose outer area revolves such that you'll have had a 360-degree view of New Orleans if you sit in the same place for 90 minutes.

The Bright Field Incident

On 14 December 1996 the freighter *Bright Field* was plying a route past the city with a load of corn when it lost all engine power. The ship was out of control, heading toward the New Orleans riverbank at Riverwalk shopping mall, where a cruise ship and a busy paddle steamer/casino were moored.

Heroic river pilot Ted Davisson, who was at the wheel, managed to maneuver between the two moored vessels but could not stop the ship from slamming into the dock, destroying 125 rooms of the Hilton Hotel and badly damaging the mall. Although 130 people were hurt, there were no fatalities. Riverwalk was closed for refurbishment until the fall of 1997. You can see press cuttings of damage and the rebuilding at a small memorial to the incident in the mall itself.

It's a great place to watch the sun set and the lights come on along the river.

Beyond the World Trade Center, the area beside the river has undergone massive redevelopment in recent years. The **Ernest N. Morial Convention Center** takes up a large lot and has attracted modern hotels to service its busy schedule. The New Orleans cruise port is also here; it sees several large vessels each week. Between the Convention Center and the Algiers ferry is **Riverwalk**, a pleasant shopping mall.

OUTLYING NEIGHBORHOODS

The French Quarter boundaries have always been sharply defined and are even more so in modern times, as the Vieux Carré Commission has been given wide-ranging power to protect the buildings of the old town but not the areas surrounding it. You can easily see the bounds of the commission's influence— highrise buildings and run-down wastelands now crowd on the Quarter's perimeter—but there are still places of interest to explore here.

The downriver boundary is marked by the Esplanade, a wide street of fine mansions separating the French Quarter from **Faubourg Marigny**

Look, it's Satchmo!— Louis Armstrong, in a park that bears his name.

(the Marigny suburb), which was planned and built to alleviate pressure as the population of the city began to grow. Faubourg Marigny has become the focus of a great deal of after-dark activity, with numerous bars and clubs. It is also a center for the gay and lesbian communities of the city.

North Rampart Street, sadly a little run down these days, marks the lakeside boundary. Where once great clubs and bars could be found, there are now only boarded-up build-

Voodoo and New Orleans

Voodoo and New Orleans seem inextricably linked through the stories of Marie Laveau, the Voodoo Queen who could control men's minds. Today you'll find voodoo dolls in most souvenir shops, and local ladies will offer to tell your fortune, claiming direct descendency from the Witch Queen herself.

The roots of voodoo can be traced back to Africa and the beliefs brought by slaves when they were transported from there to Louisiana and other European colonies. Voodoo means "spirit," and the practice of voodoo relates to the rituals involved in worship of that spirit. This often involves trance-like states in which the "worshippers" believe they are possessed by a *loa*, an intermediary to the spirit world. This leads to higher understanding or brings the answer to a problem or question. Thus priests and priestesses (women predominate in voodoo worship) are consulted about problems with health, love, and money.

The slave population gradually began to convert to Catholicism (often through coercion), but for many years Congo Square (now the site of Armstrong Park) was the center of Voodoo practice in the city. Today, some pure Voodoo temples can still be found carrying out the ancient practices.

ings. On the far side of North Rampart is **Armstrong Park**, named after the great jazz musician and son of the city. You'll find a statue of the man gracing the grassy areas and a small lake with its ducks and geese, but Pops would be saddened to know that his park can be a dangerous place. It is not advisable to visit after dark, unless you are attending a performance at the **Municipal Auditorium** or the **Theatre of Performing Arts**, which can also be found here.

Two blocks beyond Armstrong Park you'll find the simple lines of **Our Lady of Guadalupe Church**, built in 1826. At this time New Orleans was under the shadow of plague and the city fathers were unhappy about carrying victims to St. Louis Cathedral for funeral services, then through the city to the cemetery. This church was constructed just in front of the two major cemeteries for the French Quarter and still plays a part in funeral services today.

The cemeteries of New Orleans—called "cities of the dead"—are fascinating places. Because the city was built below river level it soon became clear that the ground was too waterlogged to bury bodies in it (this is true of most places in Louisiana). Instead, the dead were buried above ground, in tombs that became more ornate as the city grew richer. **St. Louis Cemetery No. 1**, found directly behind the church, contains tombs of some of the city's most influential families. Perhaps the most visited tomb here is that of Marie Laveau, the so-called Voodoo Queen who exerted a powerful influence over the city in the 19th century. People still visit to ask her help from beyond the grave; you will see fresh voodoo charms placed around her tomb. It is not advised that you explore this area alone; join one of the many enjoyable guided tours to ensure your safety.

The upriver boundary of the French Quarter is marked by **Canal Street,** named for a canal that was never actually built.

Looking at Canal Street today you will note how straight it is, and the wide median where the path of the canal would have been. Following the Louisiana Purchase in 1803, Americans began pouring into New Orleans, but the Creole population refused to let them settle in the French Quarter, so they had to settle beyond Canal. The two communities came together at the thoroughfare, and it became known to everyone as "neutral ground." Canal became the main commercial road, with large department stores catering to both communities; today many have closed due to changes in shopping habits and the creation of numerous malls. The Maison Blanche department store no longer trades, but its beautiful façade has been saved; it is being converted into a Ritz-Carlton Hotel. Unfortunately other parts of Canal Street have not fared so well. If you walk toward the river, the **Old Customs House** is on your left-hand side. When the building was completed—an amazing 65 years after it was begun—it was the largest federal building in the US after the Capitol in Washington DC. Toward the bottom of Canal Street is **Harrah's Casino**, which finally opened in late 1999 after years of financial problems.

THE CENTRAL BUSINESS DISTRICT (CBD) AND THE WAREHOUSE DISTRICT

Before the Louisiana Purchase, the upriver side of Canal Street consisted of several large plantation estates. When the American settlers began to arrive, a new town sprang up as social and administrative center for the population, and gradually the plantations were broken up and the land sold in smaller lots. Of course as the city moved into the twentieth century and building techniques changed, there was pressure to redevelop the French Quarter—the oldest part of town. Luckily, the French Quarter was saved at the eleventh hour, and therefore new building began with a vengeance in the area of town just beyond Canal. Today this part of town, called the Central Business District or CBD, is characterized by high-rise office buildings and hotels—much as many other American cities—but you can still see vestiges of "the American Quarter" hidden among the acres of glass and steel. **Poydras Street** is the main arterial route today, with many office buildings flanking the wide thoroughfare. It links directly with interstate routes. It also intersects with Loyola Avenue, where you will find City Hall, the rail and bus stations, and the main US Post Office. At the top of Poydras is the **Louisiana Superdome**, the major sporting arena for the area. Views of the Superdome dominate the CBD; it's not that it is the tallest building in the district, but rather that its bul-

There is no shortage of street musicians in the French Quarter—you will hear music everywhere you go.

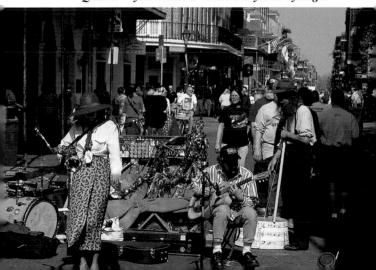

The newly revamped warehouse district boasts the Contemporary Arts Center, which showcases younger artists.

bous shape sits like a spaceship looming behind each façade. Superdome hosts all kinds of activities—the most important regular sporting event is the final of the college football competition, the Sugarbowl, in January of each year. Its stands are designed to change configuration easily to accommodate different pitches and stages, with a capacity of over 75,000 for concerts. You can tour the Superdome on most days to get "behind-the-scenes" statistics about just how big this place is—even how many lights it has.

St. Charles Avenue was the main thoroughfare of the American Quarter, and **Lafayette Square** was the Jackson Square of this community. Several beautiful buildings surround this tiny open space. On the lake side of the square is

Gallier Hall, once the old City Hall, designed by James Gallier Sr. Although no longer a public building, the traditional champagne toast between the city Mayor and the King of the Rex parade still takes place on its steps each year.

Until recently, the warehouse district was rather dormant along the riverside of the CBD, but its old abandoned warehouses, once used in river trade, have been brought back to life in the last thirty years. In 1974 a group of upcoming artists were looking for cheap studio and gallery space, and K&B, a pharmacy company, made one of their old warehouses on Camp Street available. In 1976 the **Contemporary Arts Center** (CAC) opened its doors and its success began to draw other like-minded people to the area. Since the mid 1980s, the vast footage of these large buildings has been coveted for up-market urban housing, gallery space, and assorted eateries, particularly as rents in the French Quarter rose dramatically in the same time frame. Today the Warehouse district is fashionable and draws the best artists, antique importers, and design studios—a great place to browse for serious souvenirs of your trip.

> **Have exact change ready for streetcars and buses.**

CAC makes a good starting point for a tour. It showcases the work of the latest contemporary talent, holds classes in visual arts and dance, and acts a social center for the artistic community. Across the street from the center is the **Confederate Museum**, set in the wood-lined Memorial Hall. This is the oldest museum in Louisiana, having opened in 1891. The museum displays relics of the "War of the States;" many items were donated by the Civil War soldiers who wore them, or by their families, including personal items belonging to Robert E. Lee and P. G. T. Beauregard. Over 100 Confederate flags are on display here as well.

Around the tiny hall, the home of the Ogden Museum of Southern Art is being completed. The museum showcases the history of the visual arts in the American South and makes an interesting contrast to CAC just a few steps away.

Development of commercial art galleries has centered on Julia Street (part of it is locally known as Gallery Row), but you can also find the **Children's Museum** housed in one of the old warehouses. The aim of this museum is to allow children to explore the world of science and math in fun ways. Any child can be a news anchorperson at the TV studio, or play musical instruments in the sound area. Younger visitors can explore tunnels, climb obstacles, and generally push their physical boundaries. There is also a great store on site with lots of educational toys for "kids" of all ages.

Where Julia Street meets Magazine Street, the **New Orleans School of Glassblowing and Print Making** offers the chance to watch artisans at work, or have a try for yourself. The first floor gallery sells pieces produced here.

☛ THE GARDEN DISTRICT

American settlers continued to take land upriver from the French Quarter, and their mansions were set in large gardens—in contrast to the Creole houses which only had courtyards or balconies. Thus, this area became known over time as the Garden District. The beautiful houses have remained in private hands, so few are open to the public, but a stroll along the streets of the Garden District reveals it to be one of the most beautiful suburbs in the US.

Traveling to the Garden District is also one of the highlights of any trip to New Orleans. The oldest continually working streetcar line runs along its northern boundary to the town of Carrollton 13 miles (26 km) away. The **St. Charles Streetcar** began its service in 1835 as the New Orleans and

Carrollton Railroad. It was originally powered by horse and mule but soon gave way to steam; finally it was electrified in 1893. The line starts at St. Charles Avenue and Canal, running every 15 minutes at peak hours. A ride of any length, even to the end of the line, costs the princely sum of $1.25. The streetcar route travels down Charles Street past Lafayette Square (see page 52) on the outbound journey (it travels down Carondelet on the inbound journey), reaching **Lee Circle** before continuing along Charles Avenue out of the city. Lee Circle has a statue of the famous

For architectural detail, it's hard to beat the Rival Mansion in the Garden District.

Confederate General atop a 60-ft (18-m) column. **K&B Plaza**, which sits on the circle, was built in 1963 and has a small sculpture park with several fine pieces, including works by Henry Moore and Isamu Noguchi.

Beyond the freeway bridge the architecture changes noticeably and this area, called the Lower Garden District, is a prelude to the delights that await farther along the line. The Garden District was originally part of the separate community, Lafayette City (incorporated in 1833). It was absorbed into greater New Orleans in 1852.

To alight at the best part of the Garden District take the stop after Jackson Avenue (First Street or stop 14) and walk toward the river. This is by no means a comprehensive tour but will be a useful introduction to the District. Stroll down First Street, taking in all the details of these beautiful homes, mostly constructed in the mid- to late 19th century and set in magnificent tree-lined avenues (watch your step, as many of the tree roots here break through the pavement). Classical Gothic-Revival and Italianate façades, and wrought-iron fences abound. On the corner of First Street at 2340 Prytania Street is the **Toby-Westfeldt House** (1838), said to be the oldest in the Garden District and built in "raised cottage" style. At the corner of Chestnut and First is **Brevard House** (1857) home of *Interview with a Vampire* author Anne Rice, and one of a number of properties that she owns in the area.

When you reach the Camp Street intersection you will find the **Payne-Strahan House**. It was here that president of the Confederacy, Jefferson Davis, died in 1889 after suddenly falling ill. Walk on past the Payne-Strahan House and then take a right along Third Street for more beautiful homes. At Fourth and Prytania you will find **Colonel Short's Villa**,

Casket Girls

Many shortages were problematic for the early colonists, but the one they brooded about the most was the absence of female companionship. Governor Bienville appealed to Paris, saying "send us some women." The regent Philippe soon obliged, opening the gates for 88 exportable female prisoners. However, the family tree of the French colony also includes some eminently respectable wives. A number of unblemished young middle-class ladies patriotically answered the call to join the colonists. Escorted by Ursuline nuns, they arrived carrying their trousseaus in hope chests, from which they got their name — casket girls. Within a few weeks they were all spoken for.

designed by Henry Howard, who was also responsible for Nottoway and Madewood plantation houses (see pages 69-71). Once you reach Washington Avenue you will see the walls of **Lafayette Cemetery** in front of you. The pretty tombs house the remains of some of the finest of Lafayette's citizens, yet this place is known more as the setting of many of Anne Rice's gory plots. Across the street from the cemetery, **Commanders Palace** restaurant sits in a striking Victorian mansion with a beautiful garden.

The riverside boundary of the Garden District is **Magazine Street**, an interesting collection of small Creole cottages now undergoing a renaissance with the arrival of antique shops, galleries, collectibles stores, and several good restaurants along its 7-mile (11-km) stretch (from New Orleans to Audubon Zoo).

The Garden District definitely has more to offer than this short tour; many houses have plaques on their railings giving their date and other important information, so further exploration can be done on your own.

UNIVERSITY DISTRICT TO CARROLLTON

The Garden District stretches away from New Orleans, but the younger houses built farther away from the city gen-

Explore the new shops and older ambiance that characterizes Magazine Street.

An elephant at the Audubon Zoological Gardens appears to be telling a story to an enraptured group of onlookers.

erally have less finesse than those between First and Third—although they still comprise beautiful residential areas. As it makes its way to Carrollton, the St. Charles Streetcar trundles along past several architectural gems— many of the wealthy built their homes directly on Charles Avenue, which means you can get great views without leaving your seat.

Number 3029 (corner of Eighth) is the **Van Benthuysen House** (1868), which hosted the German Consulate in the years before WWII. Number 3811 is now **The Columns Hotel**, where Louis Malle filmed scenes for *Pretty Baby*. The 1941 house at number 5705 was built as an exact replica of Tara in the film *Gone with the Wind*; number 5809, a fine white structure, has been christened "the wedding cake house" because its delicate carved balustrades and columns look like icing decoration.

The streetcar eventually reaches the university district, where two campuses sit almost side-by-side. **Loyola University** is the largest Roman Catholic university in the south and has been on this campus since 1911. **Tulane University** has strength in medical study, having developed from the Medical College of Louisiana founded in 1834.

Opposite the campus area is **Audubon Park**; you'll also alight here for the Zoological Garden. The park was the setting for the World Trade Fair of 1884, but today is a haven of peace and tranquillity—save for the sound of golf club hitting ball. The jogging/roller-blading/cycling track attracts students and local fitness fanatics, and there are wild birds to feed. Squirrels are your constant companions as you stroll through the beautiful live oaks.

Audubon Zoological Garden is a 15-minute walk through the park, or you can take one of the regular shuttle buses that link with the St. Charles Streetcar (Magazine Street bus 11 stops directly outside the zoo, with pick-ups downtown). Set in 58 acres (23 hectares) of what was an old plantation, the zoo is landscaped with enclosures including an Asian Domain with tigers and elephants; a World of Primates with orangutans, gorillas, and tamarins; and the Louisiana Swamp—a fair facsimile of the real thing, so if you don't intend to take a swamp tour, come here instead. The zoo and aquarium—as part of the Audubon Institute—both have programs contributing to efforts to conserve endangered species.

The streetcar continues on to the final part of its journey to **Carrollton**, once a separate city (a place where city dwellers would come for day-trips on Sundays) but now a suburb of New Orleans. It's a quiet place with cafés and restaurants, and very relaxing if you want to escape from the noise of the city for a while.

CITY PARK TO LAKESIDE

At 1,500 acres (600 hectares), **City Park** is one of the largest urban parks in the US. Once the site of several old plantations, including that of Louis Allard, the land was donated to the city by John McDonogh and opened in 1854. The park has some beautiful live oaks dripping with Spanish moss which became infamous in the 18th century as the setting for many duels—the standard way in which gentlemen settled matters of principle or passion. Two large trees are known as **"the Dueling Oaks"** for this reason. In the weeks leading up

City Park is home to many and varied objects of interest, including this unusual Greek-style monument, the Peristyle.

to Christmas, thousands of white lights are placed in the trees here to produce a spectacular sight—a wintry tunnel in this subtropical clime. The event has been christened **Celebration in the Oaks**.

The entrance of the park is marked by a large **statue of General P. G. T. Beauregard**, the man who ordered the shot that started the Civil War at Fort Sumpter.

Behind the statue, Lelong Drive leads to the majestic **New Orleans Museum of Art** (NOMA), also known as the Isaac Delgado Museum. The building, a true Neo-Classical structure, was completed in 1911. A Lin Avery sculpture sits above a small fountain at the entrance. The museum has a varied collection, including several Fabergé eggs created for the Romanov court in Russia. But pride of place goes to a Degas portrait of local socialite Estelle Musson dating from the 1870s, when the French painter spent several months with his uncle in New Orleans. Other collections include Dutch masters, African and pre-Columbian art, and art and furniture from throughout Louisiana.

City Park has many other delights to fill a sunny day. West of the art gallery is the **Casino Building**, not for gambling—though that was its original purpose—but now a place to obtain tickets, fishing permits, boat rentals, and refreshments. The large lake, Bayou Metairie, sits in front of this building. Facilities include a children's play area, picnic tables, and a strange Greek-temple–style edifice called the **Peristyle** that was erected in 1907. A children's fairytale theme park, **Storyland**, has a Ferris wheel and carousel rides as well as costumed staff who act out nursery rhymes and beloved children's stories. Next door are the **Botanical Gardens**, a beautiful collection of plants, fountains, and statuary built during the Great Depression as an exercise in unemployment reduction.

*The Longue Vue House is notable for the extensive
and lovingly maintained gardens that surround it.*

For those who enjoy sports, City Park has numerous
opportunities. Two 18-hole golf courses, mini-golf, tennis,
softball, and rowing are all available; obtain details from the
park itself.

Before leaving the area, head out of the front entrance and
across Bayou St. John to find **Pitot House** (1799) at 1440
Moss Street. This was the home of James Pitot, the first
mayor of the incorporated city of New Orleans (1804–1805).
St. Francis Cabrini, the first American to achieve sainthood,
bought the house later. Built in West-Indies cottage style,
this is not its original site — it was originally built at 1370
Moss Street, but it was faithfully reconstructed after it was
moved; even the fence looks two hundred years old.

East of City Park, behind St. Louis Cemetery No. 3, is the **Fairground, Racetrack, and Jazz Fest Grounds**, home to numerous events throughout the year including, obviously, the reknowned Jazz Fest in April/May of each year.

Travel west of City Park, across I10, to visit **Longue Vue House**—built for the New Orleans businessman Edgar Bloom Stern, whose wife Edith came from the Sears family. This Classical Revival mansion was completed in the 1930s. The house is filled with fine American, English, and French furniture; the surrounding 8 acres (3 hectares) of gardens designed by Ellen Biddle Shipman have several different themes, including a hands-on discovery garden created with children in mind, a working vegetable garden, useful herbs and flowers, and a butterfly garden.

City Park stretches north almost, but not quite, to **Lake Pontchartrain**, a huge lake north of the city. Its brackish water is only 15 ft (5 m) deep, yet it covers an area of over 600 square miles (1,600 sq km). The lake and lakefront parks are a favorite recreation ground for New Orleans residents, who indulge in water-skiing, sailing, and windsurfing on the lake, plus jogging, ball games, and Frisbee on the grassy lawns of the waterfront. Lakeshore Drive, running along the southern shoreline, is perfect for a leisurely drive. Look out for the **Mardi Gras Fountain**, whose jets are colored gold, green, and purple, the colors of Mardi Gras, and also for the pavilion where Pope John Paul II held an open-air mass during his visit to the city in 1987.

For many years the lake was a barrier to northward development until it was bridged in 1957. The 24-mile (38-km) **Lake Pontchartrain Causeway** is the longest bridge of its kind in the world. It is said that throughout the middle—eight miles—of the bridge it is not possible to see land either in front of or behind you.

New Orleans Highlights

Aquarium of the Americas. 1 Canal Street; Tel. (504) 861-5101; <www.auduboninstitute.com>. Daily 9:30am–5:30pm (later in summer); $11.25 adults, $5 children (see page 44).

Audubon Zoological Gardens. 6500 Magazine Street; Tel. (504) 581-4629; <www.auduboninstitute.com>. Daily 9:30am–5pm (winter), 9:30am–6pm (summer); $9 persons over 12, $4.75 children (combined tickets to Zoo, Aquarium, and cruise $28.50 and $14.25) (see page 59).

Blaine Kern's Mardi Gras World. 223 Newton Street, Algiers; Tel. (504) 361-7821. Open daily 9:30am–4:30pm; admission $11.50 adults, $8.50 children over 12. Manufacturer of Mardi Gras carnival floats and figures (see page 45).

Children's Museum. 420 Julia Street; Tel. (504) 523-1357. Tuesday–Saturday 9:30am–4:30pm (Monday summer only), Sunday noon–4:30pm; $5 for all except under one year. Interactive museum for children (see page 54).

Civil War Museum. Memorial Hall, 929 Camp Street; Tel. (504) 523-4522. 10am–4pm Monday–Saturday; admission $5 over 12. Relics of the "War of the States" (see page 69).

Gallier House. 1118–1132 Rue Royale; Tel. (504) 525-5661. Monday–Saturday 10am–4pm (last tour 3:30pm); $6, $10 for both this and Hermann-Grima House. 1857 home of James Gallier Jr., a prominent city architect (see page 34).

Hermann-Grima House. 820 St. Louis Street; Tel. (504) 525-5661; Monday–Saturday 10am–4pm (last tour 3:30pm); $6 adults, $10 for both this and Gallier House. 1831 furnished family mansion (see page 39).

Longue Vue House. 7 Bamboo Road; Tel. (504) 488-5488; web site <www.longuevue.com>. Open Monday–Saturday 10am–4:30pm, Sunday 1pm–5pm; admission $7 adults, $3 children. Historic city estate and 8 acres (3 hectares) of gardens (wheelchair-friendly) (see page 63).

Louisiana Superdome. Sugarbowl Drive; Tel. (504) 587-3803. Tours each weekday, sports schedules permitting, 10:30am, noon, and 1:30pm; admission $6 adults, $4 children 5–10 (see page 51).

Madam John's Legacy. 623 Dumaine Street; Tel. (504) 568-6968. Open Tuesday–Sunday 9am–5pm; admission $5 adults, $4 children 12–18. Historic French cottage house (see page 35).

Mardi Gras Museum at the Presbytère. 751 Chartres Street; Tel. (504) 568-6968. Open Tuesday–Sunday 9am–5pm; admission $5 adults, $4 children 12–18. Mardi Gras costumes, video of parades (see page 32).

Musée Conti Wax Museum. 917 Rue Conti; Tel. (504) 525-2605. Open daily 10am–5:30pm; admission $6.25 adults, $5.57 children. (see page 39).

New Orleans Museum of Art (NOMA). City Park; Tel. (504) 488-2631. Open Tuesday–Sunday 10am–5pm; admission $6 adults, $3 children 3–17 (see page 61).

Pitot House. 1440 Moss Street; Tel. (504) 482-0312. Open Wednesday–Saturday 10am–3pm; admission $5 adults, $3 children Historic French era colonial house (see page 62).

The Cabildo/Arsenal. 701 Chartres Street; Tel. (504) 568-6968. Open Tuesday–Friday 9am–5pm; admission $5 adults, $4 children 12–18. Louisiana State Museum; exhibits charting the history of the state (see page 30).

The Historic New Orleans Collection. 533 Rue Royale; Tel. (504) 523-4662. Tuesday–Saturday 10am–4:30pm; admission free to some galleries, $4 to others. An extensive collection of historical artifacts (see page 37).

The New Orleans Historic Voodoo Museum. 724 Dumaine Street; Tel. (504) 523-7685; web site <www.voodoomuseum.com>. Daily 10am–8pm; admission $3.60 adults, $2.25 students. Explains the basic principles of voodoo practice (see page 36).

The Old US Mint. 400 The Esplanade; Tel. (504) 568-6968. Open daily 9am–5pm; admission $5 adults, $4 children 12–18. Coin minting building, now housing the Jazz Museum (see page 43).

Top of the Mart. 33rd Floor World Trade Center, 2 Canal Street; Tel. (504) 391-3544. Open Monday–Friday 10am–midnight, Saturday 11am–1am, Sunday 2pm–midnight. Revolving lounge with panoramic views (see page 46).

EXCURSIONS

The Plantation Route—New Orleans to Baton Rouge

In the 1850s, 75% of American millionaires lived on the Mississippi River between New Orleans and Natchez (Mississippi state to the north), making an exorbitant living from huge plantations of sugar cane. They built the largest and most spectacular plantation houses in efforts to display their great wealth and to accommodate their often extremely large families—13 or more children was not unusual. Of course many houses suffered devastating damage during the War between the States, and were left to decay during the reconstruction period; often the land was sold off. Others were saved with the discovery of oil on their lands in the early part of the 20th century.

Today, the remaining ante-bellum (pre–Civil War) mansions along the river between New Orleans and Baton Rouge can be visited in a one or two-day tour, along what has been designated the Great River Route. Of course the great Mississippi has changed beyond recognition since their heyday. It is now tamed—for the most part—and its course set by controlling the flow upstream. Where once the river would have been the only way to reach the towns and cities, there are now roads; paddle steamers would make slow progress and for many plantation owners, a simple business trip to New Orleans would have involved at least one week away from home. The major role of the Mississippi in modern times is that of a trade conduit, and the focus of oil and natural gas processing from major reserves in the Gulf of Mexico. Numerous large industrial plants sit along the levees, overshadowing some of these great houses.

The well-preserved Laura Plantation gives visitors an opportunity to explore the pre–Civil War South.

The nearest plantation house to New Orleans, and also the oldest, is **Destrehan** (1787), a twenty-minute drive via the I10 and LA310. Although the wings were added in 1820 and a major renovation was undertaken as early as 1830, the construction methods and the West-Indies–style roof are unique to the house.

Take route 44 along the river to reach **San Francisco Plantation House**, the most ornate and colorful of all. Classic Creole in style, the main rooms are on the second floor (away from the water, and more likely to catch the few summer breezes). The exterior gingerbread trim work is delightful, highlighted with contrasting colors. Inside the house, the ceiling murals and faux-paint effects can be found nowhere else along the river. When San Francisco was built in 1856 it was

> **The city's name is pro-
> nounced N'Awlins—
> saying New Orleens is a
> sure-fire way to announce
> you're a visitor!**

named St. Frusquin, taken from
the French phrase *sans fruscins*
meaning "without a penny in
my pocket." It seems that the
house cost the original owner
Edmond Marmillion a little

more than he had bargained for!

To reach the next couple of houses, you'll need to cross the
river. If you're lucky you'll catch a glimpse of one of the paddle steamers that ply the route from Natchez in the north to
New Orleans.

If you cross the river via the LA641 and take a right on the
LA18, after a few minutes you will find **Laura Plantation**
on your left. Laura offers perhaps the most complete picture
of plantation life, thanks to careful research and study of the
papers left behind by Laura Locoul (now in the French
National Archives), whose family owned this plantation plus
a house in New Orleans. Laura's memoirs, painting an intimate image of plantation life at this simple Creole house, are
the basis of a fascinating guided tour, which delves deeper
into the delicate subject of slavery than any other. Laura
Plantation is also the home of the little scamp Br'er
Rabbit—African slaves brought their own folk tales with
them, which, over time, became stories of the little rabbit
and his adversary Br'er Fox.

Only five minutes away from Laura Plantation is **Oak
Alley** (1839). It is perhaps the prettiest, a charming mansion
set in verdant lawns and famed for the 28 live oaks guarding
the riverside entrance that create one of the most beautiful
images in the south, particularly as the sun sets. The oaks are
at least 250 years old and so pre-date the house. The house
is equally striking—classic revival style—and the tour, con-

ducted by hoop-skirted ladies, presents the romantic image of plantation life, which makes it an interesting contrast to Laura.

Tezcuco Plantation, built in raised-cottage style with fantastic wrought-iron supports, was completed only weeks before the start of the Civil War. Tezcuco is an Aztec Indian word meaning resting place; the owner Benjamin Tureaud had undergone a military tour of duty in Mexico before settling down to raise a family here. Although the house has been renovated several times, the chimneys that served its seven fireplaces were lost to Hurricane Betsy in 1965 and have not been replaced. Tezcuco Plantation has a small Civil War Museum and several cottages in the grounds, which offer bed-and-breakfast accomodations in rustic style.

Nearby **Houmas House** takes its name from the Houmas Indians, who used to occupy this tract of land before it was sold in 1812. The earliest part of the house, four rooms linked by a narrow corridor and outside staircase, was built during Spanish rule. In 1840 new owners had a much larger Greek-revival mansion built in front of the earlier building. In the late 18th century Houmas Plantation was the largest producer of sugar cane in the US—it actually changed hands in 1858 for one million dollars—but by the beginning of the 20th century the land had been broken up and the house fell into disrepair. In 1940, the house was bought by Dr. George Crozat of New Orleans, who restored it to its 1840 condition and used it as a weekend retreat. The formal gardens at the rear are a delight.

Across the river at White Castle is **Nottoway Plantation**. The largest of the ante-bellum homes on the river, Nottoway was completed in 1849 for John Hampden Randolph and was state-of-the-art for its time, with both indoor plumbing and gas lighting. Restoration of the 64 rooms, undertaken by the present owner, who originates from Sydney, Australia, has been ongoing since 1980. The beautiful details in marble, wood, and plaster are perhaps seen at their best in the most splendid room, the 65-ft (21-m) Grand White Ballroom. Outside, the river sits far closer to the house than during Randolph's time, evidence of the immense erosive power of the flowing water.

The final plantation house is a little off the beaten track and away from the river on Bayou Lafourche at Napoleonville. **Madewood** was designed for Thomas Pugh by renowned architect Henry Howard, and made using wood from the surrounding plantation—hence the name. The furniture, though not original to the house, is all in keeping with

The remarkably modern Nottoway Plantation
majestically stands a stone's throw from the river.

the period. Perhaps the best thing about Madewood is that you can stay the night, either in the main house or in cottages on the grounds. Have an aperitif, dinner, and coffee and brandy in the historic family rooms before heading to bed upstairs—perhaps you'll dream that the place is really yours! Oh, and Brad Pitt took time away from filming *Interview with a Vampire* to spend a weekend here. You'll find a plaque above the bed where he slept.

Baton Rouge

Following the Great River Route leads eventually to Baton Rouge, capital of Louisiana. Baton (pronounced Batten) Rouge has a population of about 400,000, yet its down-town area is small, giving the feeling of a laid-back town rather than a bustling metropolis. The city has been sus-tained by the oil industry and refining plants lie all along the river here, but Baton Rouge is also an administrative center and university town—so there are many contrasting influences mingling to produce the particular atmosphere of the place.

Baton Rouge, meaning red rod or stick, was named by the French. The Indians who held this part of the Mississippi displayed a red totem on the riverbank; French explorers and trappers would look out for the "baton rouge" as they navigated the bayous.

Baton Rouge was the home turf of Huey Long, the famous, or perhaps infamous, politician who brought numerous benefits to the people of Louisiana during his term as Governor, while salting away millions in bribes and creative accounting scams. Long was also responsible for Baton Rouge having two Capitol buildings when most states are fine with just one. **The Old Capitol Building**, a mid-19th century Gothic structure with elegant lines, was abandoned in 1931 when **The New Capitol Building** was completed. Planned and built during Long's tenure, the present building is stunning and can be seen from all around the city. Reminiscent of the Woolworth building in New York, it is the tallest capitol building in the US. The exterior is beautifully carved in Art-Nouveau style, and the interior reveals a wealth of marble and bronze. There are guided tours of the interior of the building, including the spot where Huey Long met his death in 1935 by an assassin's bullet. You will even be able to see bullet holes in the marble walls made when a hail of shots from Long's bodyguards cut down the gunman—over 40 bullets pierced his body. Long didn't travel very far to his resting place. The beautiful formal gardens in front of the capitol surround his tomb, which is topped by a statue of the great man looking toward the building he loved.

The *U.S.S. Kidd*, a restored Navy destroyer that served in both WWII (it was damaged in battle at Okinawa by a kamikaze pilot) and the Korean conflict, is open for tours. The ship is one of several war relics, including an E-7E Corsair aircraft used in the Vietnam war, which together act as a memorial to Louisiana's Veterans.

Cajun Country

In south Louisiana, land of the cypress swamps, live a group of people whose language and lifestyle makes them unique in American society. Known as the Cajuns, they still revere the cuisine, music, and life of the land that their forefathers developed. The Cajuns are descended from Frenchmen who set out from their native land in the early 1600s to start a new life in the French colony of what is now eastern Canada. They named their new homeland Acadia and prospered in the natural abundance as fishermen, trappers, and farmers.

*Born on the bayou: The sun setting through cypress trees
is symbolic of the resilient Cajun culture.*

It is only in the 20th century that Cajuns have opened up
their society a little to welcome outsiders. Despite not being
able to speak their native tongue in schools, this language
has survived, as has their distinctive music and their irre-
pressible *joie de vivre*. In 1969 the Council for the
Development of French in Louisiana (CODOFIL) was inaugurated, and community pride has since risen to new heights.
Today throughout Cajun country there are fêtes, festivals,
and community get-togethers where everyone can *fais-do-
do*, which is Cajun for "have a great time."

Our journey through Cajun country leads in an arc west of
Baton Rouge to Lafayette and counter-clockwise south, back
toward New Orleans. To fully appreciate the area, it is imper-

ative to journey along the smaller routes rather than on the interstate—the newly designated I49 (currently being upgraded) cuts through the region.

The unofficial capital of Cajun country is **Lafayette**, less than two hours from New Orleans by interstate. The offices of CODOFIL are here, and the city posts signs in both English and French to remind locals and visitors of the Cajun tradition. Head to the **Lafayette Museum** at 1122 Lafayette Street for a comprehensive introduction to Cajun history and lifestyle; follow this with a visit to **Vermilionville** near the airport, a Cajun theme park where a number of 18th-century buildings have been moved to one site beside a bayou, then complimented by faithful reconstructions that show how an early Cajun community might have lived. The staff are happy to share their knowledge about the Cajun way of life. The barn has a small stage hosting live music every day; visit on the weekends to watch locals join in the dancing.

North of Lafayette, near the northern border of Cajun country in prairie country, lies the small town of Eunice. The

Freebooters

Jean Lafitte and his brother Pierre ran an empire deep in the bayou country near New Orleans, based on what some called piracy, though the charge was never proven in court. When, in 1813, Governor Claiborne offered $500 for Jean Lafitte's capture, the insolent rogue reacted by offering $1,500 for the capture of Claiborne. In 1814 the two privateers were overcome by patriotism. They volunteered their inside knowledge of the bayou country, helping General Jackson plan his tactics against the British in the Battle of Orleans, for which Jackson won them a full pardon.

Fais-do-do: A Cajun band and dancers step to the beat of the rhythm at a festival in Cajun country.

Jean Lafitte Prairie Acadian Cultural Center in the heart of town depicts life in this area—different from the more southern Cajun community where residents live in the swamps. Musical traditions are strong here and there are several clubs, but the Saturday-night performances of live Cajun music at the **Liberty Theatre** are the highlight of the week. **Rendezvous des Cajuns** is a showcase of Cajun music featuring new and established bands. As soon as the music starts, the audience wastes no time in leaving their seats, and everybody—aged 5 to 80—takes to the dance floor. You'll hear the centuries-old Cajun French being spoken, though most Cajuns also speak English fluently. If you can't make the performance at Eunice (6pm), listen to it on the radio.

You'll miss the best of the action, but you'll still be able to enjoy the music.

Breaux Bridge, arguably the earliest Cajun settlement, is now a sleepy town set on the Bayou Teche. A burgeoning artistic community and several antique stores make it worth a stop at any time of year, but most people know the settlement for its annual Crawfish Festival (held on the first full weekend in May) when the population increases four-fold to sample huge amounts of what can be called the Cajun country's national food.

Traveling south following Bayou Teche leads to **St. Martinville**, a beautiful little historic town. The downtown area is kept neat as a pin, with communal gardens along the water's edge; St. Martin de Tours Catholic Church looks as if the paint on its clapboards has just dried. Behind the church is the **Acadian Memorial**, a small museum dedicated to the ancestors of today's Cajuns; an eternal flame burns in their memory, and a Wall of Names records every individual for posterity. For those who want to learn more about Cajun life, the museum also has a multi-media archive to explore. Next to the Memorial Hall you will find what local people call "the most photographed tree in America." The huge, live **Evangeline oak** is said to be the tree under which Henry Wordsworth Longfellow's Acadian heroine *Evangeline* met her long-lost lover. Here you can sit and watch the bayou water flow by and enjoy the peace and quiet.

The settlement of **New Iberia** is known more or less worldwide, for its name appears on the label of every bottle of Tabasco sauce, which is produced in a factory at nearby **Avery Island**. You can tour the sauce-bottling factory of McIlhenny and Co. every day; the tours are free. The company also operates a 200-acre (81-hectare) **Jungle Park** with numerous species of native animals and a 20,000-member colony of snowy egrets, which gives the park its local nickname, Bird City.

In downtown New Iberia, sitting on the banks of the bayou, is a Greek-revival plantation house called **Shadows-on-the-Teche** (1834). Displayed inside is a collection of 17,000 family documents, for added interest; having been lost for decades, these were found locked in over 40 trunks in the attic.

South of New Iberia, where the waters of the Mississippi fan out into a huge delta and begin their final journey to mix with the seawater of the Gulf of Mexico, is swampland. The Cajuns here have a different lifestyle from those in the north, based on hunting and trapping and still reliant on the sea and crawfish catches. At Thibodaux, on Bayou Lafourche at 314 St. Mary Street, you will find the **Jean Lafitte Wetlands Acadian Cultural Center**, sister to the Prairie Center at Eunice (see page 75). Here you will be able to explore the culture and practices of the wetland Acadians. There are also numerous boat tours in the region; though the landscape has changed a great deal with the taming of the Mississippi, the swamps are still wild and beautiful places, with a wealth of wildlife to see—from alligators to nutria, birds, fish, and sometimes deer. **The Wildlife Gardens** at Gibson have a host of native creatures and exotic birds in a swampland area specially adapted so that people can enjoy foot access; you can see alligators, deer, wading birds, and wild boar. Wildlife Gardens also takes in injured animals, rehabilitating them when possible. And if you would like to try your hand at living on the bayou, you can stay overnight in one of the "Cajun shacks" here—you won't need to catch your own breakfast, as it is provided in the on-site café every morning.

Highlights Beyond New Orleans

Acadian Memorial. 121 New Market Street, St. Martinville; Tel. (337) 394-2258; <www.acadianmemorial.org>. Daily 10am–4pm; $2 adults, $1 school-age children (see page 76).

Destrehan Plantation. 13034 River Road, Destrehan; Tel. (504) 764-9315. Open daily 9:30am–4pm; admission $8 adults, $4 children 13–17, $2 children 6–12 (see page 67).

Houmas House. 40136 Highway 942, Burnside, Darrow; Tel. (225) 473-7841; <www.houmashouse.com>. Daily 10am–4pm (November–January) 10am–5pm (February– October); admission $8 adults, $6 children 13–17, $3 children 6–12 (see page 69).

Laura Plantation. 2247 Highway 18, Vacherie; Tel. (225) 265-7690. Open daily 9:30am–5pm; admission $8 adults, $4 children 6–17 (see page 68).

Nottoway Plantation. 30970 Mississippi River Road, White Castle; Tel. (225) 545-2730. Daily 9am–5pm. $8 adults, $3 children under 13 (see page 69).

Oak Alley Plantation. 3645 Highway 18, Vacherie; Tel. (225) 265-2151; web site <www.louisianatravel.com/oak_alley>. Open daily 9am–5pm (5:30pm March–October); admission $8 adults, $3 children 6–12 (see page 68).

San Francisco Plantation House. Highway 44, Reserve; Tel. (504) 535-2341; web site <www.sanfranciscoplantation.org>. Open daily 10am–4pm (4:30pm Mar–Oct); admission $8 adults, $4 children 13–17, $3 children 6–12 (see page 67).

Shadows-on-the-Teche. 317 Main Street, New Iberia; Tel. (318) 369-6446. Open daily 9am–4:30pm; admission $6 adults, $3 children 6–11 (see page 77).

Tezcuco Plantation. 3138 Highway 44, Darrow; Tel. (225) 562-3929. Open daily 9am–5pm; admission $8 adults, $6 children 13–17, $3 children 6–12 (see page 69).

U.S.S. Kidd. 305 South River Road, Baton Rouge; Tel. (504) 342-1942. Open daily 9am–5pm; admission $6 adults, $3.50 children under 12 (see page 72).

Vermilionville. 1600 Surrey Street, Lafayette; Tel. (318) 233-4077. Open daily 10am–5pm; admission $8 adults, $5 children 6 and over (see page 74).

WHAT TO DO

The "What to Do" in New Orleans is probably of equal importance to "Where to Go" in its effect on your overall vacation experience. More than most other destinations, nightlife and entertainment have much more of an influence on your perception of the place. If you stay in your room after dark or leave venues early in the evening, you're going to miss a huge part of the essence of New Orleans.

FESTIVALS

Mardi Gras

The largest festival in North America, Mardi Gras is one of the must-see events in the world. Although known for its fancy parades, masks, beads, and more risqué elements, the celebration of Mardi Gras or Fat Tuesday has its origins in pre-Christian times. The pagan celebrations of the end of winter were fused with Christian beliefs from the earliest days; Mardi Gras marks the last day before the beginning of Lent (when one

> **Don't forget to shout "throw me something, Mister" as the parade passes by—shrinking violets get no beads!**

gives up one's pleasures until Easter). The French brought the celebration of Mardi Gras with them when they settled in Louisiana, and although the celebration waned in popularity at the beginning of the 19th century, it was resurrected and gradually developed into the mega-celebration that it is today.

Mardi Gras is actually the culmination of a carnival season (the word carnival is derived from a Latin phrase which means "farewell to the flesh") which begins after Twelfth Night, on 6 January each year. For wealthy and influential

New Orleans natives it is a time of lavish parties and other social events, including the introduction of debutantes into society. All these activities are still very important to New Orleans families, but they take place in relative privacy. However, the parades, perhaps the most obvious manifestation of Mardi Gras to the outsider, have become much more open in the last few decades. The floats seem to get more outrageous every year (many of the best cost over $500,000 each), as do the costumes. Standing in the crowds and having a good time is, of course, open to everyone!

This Krewe member is demure compared to other Mardi Gras revelers.

The final two weeks before Fat Tuesday see a build-up in activity and excitement. Everyone decorates their homes with masks, ribbons, and flags in Mardi Gras colors. Parades increase in frequency in these last two weeks, each being bigger, more lavish, and more ornately decorated than the last.

Arthur Hardy's Mardi Gras Guide is probably the best guide to the parade season, with parade routes and times. You can find it in stores across the city, or pre-order your copy: Arthur Hardy Enterprises Inc.; Tel. (504) 838-6111; fax (504) 838-0100; web site <www.mardigrasguide.com>.

Since 1935, **Spring Fiesta** allows visitors to enter some of the historic homes of New Orleans and Louisiana not ordinarily open to the public. There is also a parade in New Orleans featuring people dressed as historic figures. For further details contact the Spring Fiesta Association, 826 St. Ann Street, New Orleans, LA 70116; Tel. (504) 581-1367.

Held in mid-April, the **French Quarter Festival** celebrates the food and music of the city with outdoor concerts and jam sessions, plus a huge cook-out at Jackson Square catered by the best restaurants in the city.

ENTERTAINMENT

Nightlife

New Orleans is literally a city that never closes; there are no local bylaws that limit club or bar hours. This means that whatever the time of day or night you can catch a live performance somewhere in town. They say that jazz was invented in New Orleans, in the narrow alleys around Basin Street when Storyville was at its height. Where these seeds were sown there have been many harvests, and the city has, over the years, given the world some of the most famous proponents of the art of syncopation—from Louis Armstrong to the Marsalis family, Harry Connick Jr. to the Neville Brothers.

Although the city has cleaned up its image since the Vieux Carré Commission was set up to protect the French Quarter, its music is still the steamiest around, from low-down blues to Dixieland to rock. A walk down Bourbon Street is a great introduction to what's available around the city. Many venues have live music booming out through the open windows and doorways into the street—though the bars are dominated by rock and blues rather than jazz. Busking musicians sit on street corners with a clarinet or trumpet in the hope of collecting your dollars and cents.

For jazz try **Palm Court Jazz Café**, 1204 Decatur Street; Tel. (504) 525-0200; **or Donna's Bar and Grill**, 800 North Rampart Street; Tel. (504) 569-6914. **Storyville** is a new venue on Bourbon that attempts to bring back the atmosphere of classic New Orleans jazz to the rock-dominated scene; Tel. (504) 410-1000. **Tipitina's** was so successful in its original venue at 501 Napoleon Avenue (Tel. 504/895-9564) that it has opened up on North Peter Street in the French Quarter (Tel. 504/566-7095). You can keep up to date with their booked acts at <www.tipitinas.com>. The club showcases anything from jazz and blues to rock music.

Blues music can be appreciated at the aptly named **House of Blues**, 225 Decatur Street; Tel. (504) 529-2624. They also have a Gospel Brunch on Sundays.

Beyond Bourbon and the French Quarter there are several other major venues for live music. At **Snug Harbor Jazz Bistro**, 625 Frenchmen Street in the Faubourg Marigny (Tel. 504/949-0696), you are most likely to catch the influence of one of the Marsalis family. Pete Fountain still plays regularly at his own venue at the **Hilton** on Poydras Street. The **Red Room** at 2040 St. Charles Avenue (Tel. 504/528-9759) offers dinner, live music, and dancing the way it used to be. This is the place to dress up and be seen! **Mid City Lanes Rock and Bowl** is a bowling alley and club combined, with zydeco and rock music. Find it at the end of the St. Charles Streetcar route, 4133 South Carrollton Avenue; Tel. (504) 482-3133.

It's not just New Orleans that has a rich musical vein. There may be something in the Mississippi water that imparts a love of music throughout the delta. There are musical instruments, and resulting rhythms and cadences, unique to each community in the state. Over time these have combined into a number of exiting musical forms. The French Acadian settlers brought simple country rhythms and the banjo, accordion, and triangle. These Cajun tunes had traditional themes of lost love, poverty, and social injustice with the lyrics in French. Other tunes were made for dancing. African slaves imported by the colonists brought their own strong rhythms and beats, often with lower bass notes, which gradually developed into musical genres like the blues. African themes also mixed with Cajun music to create Zydeco, the rhythm of the blues combined with Cajun accordion cadences. The name is thought to

A saxophone player in the French Quarter shares his craft with all who pass by.

come from the French word for beans, *les haricot*, which changed phonetically over the years. The lyrics can be in French or a mix of French and English.

Out of the city, try the following venues for live Cajun or Zydeco music: **Mulate's Breaux Bridge**, 325 Mill's Avenue, Breaux Bridge (Tel. 337/332-4648); **Prejean's Restaurant**, 3480 Interstate Highway 49 North, Lafayette (Tel. 318/896-3247; web site <www.prejeans.com>); **Rendez-vous des Cajuns**, Liberty Theatre, 200 Park Avenue, Eunice (Tel. 337/457-7839).

For an overall understanding of the music scene in Louisiana, try the web site <www.louisianaradio.com>, where you can listen to a range of local musical forms.

Theatre and the Arts

New Orleans has been a center of the arts since Marquis de Vaudreuil became Governor of this French colony in 1743. The opera society and a ballet company (run along with the Cincinnati Ballet Company) both stage performance seasons during the year.

Performances take place at the **Mahalia Jackson Theatre of the Performing Arts** at 801 North Rampart Street on the edge of the French Quarter; Tel. (504) 565-7470. Call for program details. The theatre also hosts pop concerts and boxing matches. The **New Orleans Municipal Auditorium** nearby at 1201 St. Peter Street hosts a wide range of performances including traveling company plays. Program information can be obtained by calling the same number as the Mahalia Jackson Theatre above. The **Saenger Theatre** at 143 North Rampart Street (box office; Tel. 504/524-2490, executive office; Tel. 504/525-1052) has recently undergone a total renovation, so it may be worthwhile to buy a ticket just to get a glimpse of the sumptuous interiors. **CAC** at 900 Camp Street has two theatres featuring theatre and dance. It fosters the work of experimental artists; Tel. (504) 523-1216 for program details. **Le Petit Théâtre du Vieux Carré** is an amateur theatre group—the oldest in America—holding a yearly program of performances in the winter months; Tel. (504) 522-2081 for next year's program.

Other Entertainment

Natchez is the origin for daily **jazz cruises** down the Mississippi. The afternoon cruise, departing at 11:30am and

Bally's Casino Paddle Steamer on Lake Ponchartrain offers another excellent way to spend an evening.

2:30pm, costs $14.75 for adults, $7.25 for children 6–12; with lunch $20.70/$13.20. The dinner cruise departs at 6pm; cruise only costs $23.50 for adults, $11.75 for children 6-12; with dinner $43.50/$21.75. There are a number of combination tickets available (in conjunction with Grey Line Tours) that offer a better value; Tel. (800) 233-2628 (toll-free in US), (504) 586-8777; fax (504) 587-0708; web site <www. steamboatnatchez.com>.

Tours of the Superdome are offered weekdays 10:30am, noon, and 1:30pm; Tel. (504) 587-3808 for further details.

The best swamp-tour operator is **Dr. Wagner's Honey Island Swamp Tours**; qualified wetland ecologist Dr. Paul Wagner, who travels as carefully as possible through the swamp, personally narrates the two-hour tours. Pick-up is available from the city, but they do not accept credit card payments; Tel. (504) 641-1769; fax (504) 643-3960.

SPORTS

Spectator Sports

The **Louisiana Superdome**, completed in 1975, plays host to several major sporting events each year and acts as a state stadium for many local sporting games. Arguably the most important for New Orleans sports fans is the Sugarbowl. New Orleans' oldest sporting event, dating from 1935, pits two college football teams against each other. The stadium has also hosted the prestigious Superbowl, which has come to New Orleans eight times in recent years. The arena has been designed to host events for different sports as well; these have included Olympic track and field trials and basketball tournaments.

The **Fair Ground Track**, 1751 Gentilly Boulevard, has been the venue for New Orleans horse racing since 1872. The main races take place through the fall and winter beginning at Thanksgiving; Tel. (504) 944-5515 for card details.

Participant Sports

There are several golf courses in the New Orleans area. Perhaps the most accessible is **Audubon Golf Club** at Audubon Park, which can be reached almost directly from the St. Charles Streetcar. Fees are $9 weekdays, $12 weekends, cart rental $11 for a single golfer. Open 6am–6:30pm; Tel. (504) 865-8260. There is only one 18-hole course at Audubon Park, but there are four at **City Park**, so on busy days you may have more opportunities here. Fees range from $9–$17 with cart rental $18. Open 5:30am–6:30pm; Tel. (504) 483-9397. New Orleans Metropolitan Convention and Visitors Bureau (NOMCVB) have published a comprehensive leaflet entitled *Bogeys on the Bayou*, listing private and public golf courses in the region. Contact them for a copy.

New Orleans is well-equipped for many other participant sports, including tennis at City Park, sailing, windsurfing, and water-skiing at Lake Pontchartrain, and jogging, roller-blading, cycling, canoeing, and fishing at City Park and Audubon Park.

The city is a great place for walking, and a pair of comfortable shoes should be at the top of your packing list. Of course the French Quarter is best seen on foot, but beyond this, the city of-

Easy does it—a golfer concentrates on his game at the Audubon Park Golf Club.

fers many other opportunities to get out into the fresh air. You can take one of the numerous guided walks through either the old or new town. All tour companies employ well-informed guides, some quirky, some serious, to enlighten you about the buildings, the people who lived in them, and the sort of activities they were up to. **New Orleans Historic Walking Tours** is excellent, run by Robert Florence, an expert on the city (see page 116). **Friends of the Cabildo** offer a two-hour walking tour of the French Quarter which includes admission to two house museums (see page 116).

Power-walking or strolling is enjoyable in both City Park and Audubon Park, where you can enjoy miles of paths through the aging oaks, stop for a picnic, watch the squirrels playing, and feed the ducks. The climate in New Orleans is conducive to this sort of activity for most of the year.

SHOPPING

New Orleans is a shopper's paradise, with hundreds of specialty shops selling all manner of interesting and unique items that make great souvenirs. These are interspersed with great restaurants, cafés, and bars, so you can relax and have a snack and drink when you feel tired.

Where to Shop

You don't need to make a special effort to find shopping in the French Quarter. Simply walking the streets will bring you into contact with hundreds of stores in the historic buildings and courtyards. **French Market** has a range of goods, the **Farmers' Market** area has superb fresh produce in season, and the **Flea Market** sells handicrafts as well as the antiques of tomorrow.

If it's raining or cool, central New Orleans has three covered malls where you can shop in comfort. The **Jax Brewery** building (where you will also find a Tourist Information Center), between the river and Jackson Square, offers numerous souvenir shops. **Riverwalk** can be found at Spanish Plaza, upriver of the Canal Street ferry terminal. It has a greater range of stores and a large eating area. Just a little way up Canal Street from Riverwalk is **Canal Place**. It classes itself as a fashion mall, with several up-market national chain stores.

Magazine Street runs from the downtown area to Audubon Zoo, and its 6 miles (10 km) of pretty Creole cottages are becoming a haven for galleries, design studios, and funky collection stores. The Magazine Street Merchants Association produces a leaflet entitled *Shoppers Dream*, which pinpoints the location of each store, restaurant, and bar for the interested visitor.

The French Market is a superb place to find what you need, with a selection ranging from antiques to trinkets.

What to Buy

Antiques. The European connection is still alive and well in New Orleans, with many dealers importing pieces from France and England. Prices are high but the quality and range is excellent, with numerous shops to explore in the French Quarter. Royal Street is the heart of the antique area, and Julia and Magazine streets have several important stores. Dealers have a great deal of expertise and will be able to give you good advice.

Arts and crafts. There are numerous galleries in the city selling both imported art and the work of local artists—the beauty of the architecture here inspires work in many materials from oil, watercolor, and acrylic to bronze, steel, and glass. You'll find several galleries in the French Quarter, along Royal and Chartres streets in particular. The Contemporary Arts Center (CAC) showcases all genres of visual art, with developing artists being particularly prominent.

Books. With the wealth of literary talent that has called the city home, it's no surprise that books are a good option here. You can purchase new books at several large stores in town or browse the antiquarian book shops for a rare edition or something that takes your fancy.

New books in favor at the moment include anything by Anne Rice, of *Interview with a Vampire* fame. All her plots are set in New Orleans, so it's interesting to follow her characters around the city. New Orleans cooking is also popular. Celebrity chefs Paul Prudhomme, Emeril Lagrasse, *et al* let us in on the secrets of their success. And of course beautiful souvenir photo-guides of the Crescent City itself, come in all price ranges.

Edibles. New Orleans produces a range of edible souvenirs, which can make great souvenirs for you or presents for the folks back home. Cajun spices are particularly popular, including the famed McIlhenny Tabasco sauce. Paul Prudhomme has de-

veloped a range of spices to help the home-chef create authentic Cajun cuisine. Hand-made pralines, chocolates, and fudge are available in pretty tins. You can also find pre-packed crawfish, soft-shelled crabs, and other seafood. Try the Farmers' Market in the French Market complex for whatever is fresh and in season.

The Flea Market offers all sorts of strange and interesting items.

Mardi Gras souvenirs. Visitors can buy beads, masks, and dolls all year round, so there's no worry about missing out on the fun. These are budget-priced souvenirs, well within a small child's buying power, which allows them to have fun shopping with the adults.

Music. This is really the place to buy jazz, blues, Cajun, and zydeco music. The Jazz Museum has a good selection in its gift shop, but there are several other specialty music shops in the downtown area, along with large chain stores in the Jax Center and at Riverwalk.

Not for everyone. Some souvenirs can be a matter of personal taste. Stuffed alligator heads of all sizes peer from the shelves of Cajun stores—or you can buy their teeth loose or set on necklaces. Voodoo amulets, dolls, and *gris-gris* bags are considered fun by non-believers—and everyone can make use of a little touch of the good luck they are meant to bestow. Or you can buy T-shirts with numerous slogans from the risqué to the downright obscene. Remember: this is New Orleans, where just about anything goes!

Tax-Free Shopping

Louisiana charges 9% sales tax on the majority of purchases, but has a scheme under which visitors from outside the US can reclaim this money (though not taxes on services such as meals and hotel rooms). All purchases must be made at participating stores—they should display a round sticker in the doorway or at payment points—and you must carry your passport and declare that you want to reclaim the tax. The vendor will complete a tax refund voucher and attach it to your receipt. You must keep these safe until you make your claim.

There are three claim points in Louisiana, but the most sensible one is at New Orleans International Airport (located next door to the post office). They will process your vouchers and issue a refund minus a handling fee. Refunds of under $500 will be issued in cash, anything larger by check mailed to your home address. You can also claim by mail. For more details, look at the web site <www.louisianataxfree.com> or call the Tax Free office; Tel. (504) 568-5323.

ACTIVITIES FOR CHILDREN

A lot of activities in New Orleans could be a little wearing for children, but it's still possible to fill their day and then leave them with a babysitter to enjoy the night-life yourself without worry. Below are a few suggestions, in no particular order, to help use up their excess energy:

Take a tour of the Vieux Carré in an open horse-drawn carriage. They'll love being the center of attention, and sitting above the action will give them a better view of the city.

A ride on the St. Charles Streetcar is fun—especially with all the clunking and clanging. Go to the end of the line just to have the pleasure of riding back to town again.

Take a steamboat ride on the river, but prepare young ears for the sound of the whistle—it really is ear-splitting!

The Children's Museum has lots of exciting experiments and hands-on activities to keep children of all ages occupied.

Audubon Zoological Gardens has a whole range of animals to enjoy. The elephant show is enjoyable and educational—it currently runs at 11:30, but call ahead for times.

The Aquarium with its huge fish, sharks, and a couple of playful sea otters will keep their attention. They can even pat a baby shark!

Swamp Tours bring home the reality of the alligators, nutria, and birds that live in the Louisiana swamps. Children love spotting the animals in their natural habitats.

City Park and Audubon Park are great places to let off steam. Take a football or Frisbee, feed the squirrels and the ducks, or climb the majestic branches of the giant old oaks.

Shopping: Even the most meager allowance will allow children to take home a souvenir. Mardi-Gras beads and masks are available all year, along with posters for bedroom walls.

If this isn't enough to keep your young ones occupied, NOCVB (New Orleans Convention and Vistors' Bureau) print a leaflet entitled *More Than 100 Things for Kids* with many more ideas about how to fill your days.

A special word about

A girl and a baby, festooned with beads, enjoy themselves at the Mardi Gras parade.

Mardi Gras and children—although much of the "naughty" behavior is definitely not for kids and the crowds can be overbearing, there really is nothing better than a parade with floats and costumes to spark a child's imagination. Just plan where you'll be in the crowd ahead of time so they can get a great view. Consult the Mardi Gras march routes, get there early, and have toys to play with and lots of snacks to keep hunger pangs at bay during your wait. And don't forget to take some bags with you so you can carry all those beads back to your hotel.

Calendar of Events

Not many New Orleans festivals are date-specific; they change depending on the year, but fall within the same month each year. There is sure to be something happening during your visit, so check with the New Orleans Convention and Visitors Bureau for comprehensive details. Listed below are the major events.

January *Jan 8th and 9th:* Reenactment of the battle of New Orleans at Chalmette battlefield. The *Sugar Bowl Classic*: college football final with a plethora of associated activities.

March *Mardi Gras, Black Heritage Festival, St. Patrick's Day Parade, Tennessee Williams Festival.Spring Fiesta, Louisiana Crawfish Festival.*

April The *French Quarter Festival, New Orleans Jazz and Heritage Festival, Crescent City Classic* road race.

May The *Greek Festival*: culture, food, and music from the classical European culture. *Breaux Bridge Crawfish Festival.*

June The *Great French Market Tomato Festival* and *The Reggae Riddums Festival*, with Caribbean food, music, and attitude.

July *4th of July:* "Go 4th on the River" street party, *New Orleans Food and Wine Experience.*

August *Louisiana Shrimp and Petroleum Festival.*

October *New Orleans Film and Video Festival, Halloween.*

December *Celebration in the Oaks*: the oaks of City Park are bedecked with lights. *New Year's Eve*: huge street parties all across the city; people gather in Jackson Square to welcome the new year.

EATING OUT

New Orleans, famed as the culinary capital of the United States, is one destination where you need to forget your waistline and simply immerse yourself in the extraordinary opportunities available to excite your taste buds. It is said that even on a long weekend one can easily gain five pounds. It won't surprise you at all when you see what's available and how huge the portions are. It's impossible to get a light snack in New Orleans; even the most humble of dishes becomes a feast.

The city's legacy of culinary delights stems from the amazing mixture of influences that come together here. French techniques, African ingredients, Spanish touches, and local bounties all meld together in this unique cuisine.

You will see two names often as you tour the restaurants, Creole and Cajun. People often get confused about what the two mean, and actually, in terms of ingredients and cooking methods, there are few differences. What separates the two is that Creole claims its roots from France and its city-dwelling settlers with their expensive imported spices, and Cajun cooking originates in the countryside—from what was grown on family farms or caught in nets or traps. Where Creole is urbane, Cajun is home-style.

Even given this culinary melting pot, the few truly fine restaurants in New Orleans are each run by one of several families who have developed cooking dynasties or nurtured chefs who have then gone on to make their own mark. Brennan's, Arnaud's, Antoine's, and Galatoire's have all been in operation for three or more generations, and each still has a high reputation. But no one stands on their laurels here, and new, exciting restaurants are always ready to step in should standards slip.

Even if you travel to New Orleans on a budget, you should have one meal in a silver-service restaurant. When a handful of the best restaurants in the US are within a short stroll of

> **Pack a jacket for dinner at fine restaurants.**

each other, it is obvious that this is an important part of the New Orleans experience, one you shouldn't miss. Food is not an interruption to your itinerary; it is an attraction in itself.

Being a 24-hour-a-day city, it should come as no surprise that you can also eat any time you want, however that doesn't mean you'll have a full choice of dining experiences late into the night. There are many places to take an early or late American breakfast, cheaper than many hotels, or head to one of the "breakfast-brunch" places, such as Brennan's, for a luxury start to the day. Lunch usually runs from 11:30am–2pm and most of the finer establishments have good value lunch menus to try. Dinner begins around 5:30pm (don't forget that most Americans eat early) and the better restaurants will stop filling tables by 10:30pm. After 11pm you'll find fast food is the only option available. Don't despair though—in New Orleans even this is a step above the ordinary.

Seafood

Crawfish or crayfish are the basis of many local dishes, both Creole and Cajun, because they are found in abundance on the bottom of the bayous in the swampland all around New Orleans. They look like miniature lobsters; you can find them plain, deep fried—you'll have great fun pulling off the heads and squeezing out the fleshy tail—or in a thick gumbo (something between a soup and a stew).

You will find shrimp as well, fried, broiled, and in salads and sandwiches. Oysters are also plentiful and delicious;

Many visitors become addicted to crawfish, which serves as a basis for many of New Orleans' most distinctive dishes.

Oysters Rockefeller was, after all, invented here. Locals love to eat them raw and order them shucked at the table—with ice-cold beer this is a veritable feast.

Blue crabs, perhaps the *piece de resistance,* are shipped from here to restaurants all over the country. Crab is served in the shell or is added to other ingredients to create signature Louisiana dishes.

In a river system as expansive as the Mississippi, and with its proximity to the Gulf of Mexico, it would be surprising if fish wasn't a major part of the diet. Catfish, flounder, speckled trout, and snapper all come, depending on the season, with a range of delicious sauces, topped with a crispy coating of almonds or pecans, or blackened by coating in spices and searing on a grill so that the outside is charred but the inside stays moist.

Meat

In the early days of settlement, meat was often preserved rather than eaten fresh, and spicy sausages are still the basis of many dishes. You may see it advertised as *andouille,* filled with spiced meat, or *boudin,* a sausage of ground pork, onions, and rice.

Once settlers began to hunt on their lands, they found deer to be the most plentiful source of meat; to this day venison is popular on menus all over the city. Along with the obviously less exotic standards, boar is also offered and, occasionally, alligator.

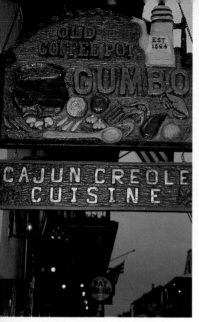

This restaurant sign advertises gumbo, a renowned Creole creation.

Local Specialties

Gumbo is a thick soup or stew made with a *roux* (a sauce made of fat and flour) and whatever other ingredients are at hand, including meat, fish, and vegetables. *Filé* gumbo, made with okra and a spice related to sassafras, is the most famous of gumbo combinations. Gumbo is always served over a portion of boiled rice. You'll find that the recipe is slightly different at every restaurant because everyone has their own favorite way of preparing it. Jambalaya, basically rice cooked in a spicy tomato sauce, is another dish that can be made up of many different ingredients and thus may be slightly different in every establishment. To this foundation add spicy sausage, chicken, shrimp, or ham along with any number of vegetables for a delicious and filling meal. Beans and

Americans call their main course an entrée. Starters are called appetizers.

rice is a simple dish descended directly from the Caribbean, the staple diet of many poor families in times gone by. *Etoufee* (pronounced ey-too-fay) means smothered, referring to a spicy, tomato-based sauce in which various ingredients are cooked and served—crawfish or shrimp etoufee are the most common.

Snack Foods

Mufulletta—it's a sandwich, but boy, what a sandwich: a Frisbee-sized round bread loaf filled with Italian sausage, ham, cheeses, and topped with chopped olives, onions, and peppers. The ubiquitous Po-boy is another special take on the sandwich, with fried clams, shrimp, or just about any other filling you'd want served on a sub roll or French bread, and usually accompanied by a full salad and numerous pickles. The word Po-boy comes from the time of the Great Depression, when bread filled with whatever was available was the only food thousands of poor boys could afford. The name stuck, but has been softened by many years of pronunciation in the rolling Louisiana dialect.

With all the excellent eateries around it is almost a surprise to encounter another New Orleans tradition—the popular Lucky Dog stalls. A whole clutch of them can be found on street corners in the French Quarter. While possibly the perfect answer to an attack of the munchies at 3am, you can order a hot dog or hamburger any time of day to eat while exploring.

Desserts

No matter how much you've eaten already, it is imperative that you make room for dessert. Bananas Foster, invented by Brennan's but served all across town, is a luscious mix of bananas sautéed with sugar and then flambéed in brandy before being served over vanilla ice cream. The local crème brulée is also exceptional—creamy, light, and the perfect finish to a heavy meal. Bread pudding is another simple dish brought to life with imaginative use of dried fruits, liquor, and spices.

Through the summer months, when the weather is hot and oppressive, restaurants will come to your aid by serving refreshing fresh fruit, ice cream, frozen yogurt, or sorbet as a finale to your meal.

Drinks

The cocktail was born in New Orleans, and any number of special drinks have been created here. During the golden age

Café au lait and beignets provide the perfect start to the day —what it lacks in nutrition, it makes up with its charm.

of Jazz the prevailing favorite was the mint julep; today it is the Hurricane, created at Pat O'Brien's Bar with rum and a mixture of tropical juices, that everyone rushes to try.

Although it isn't a long drink, and therefore not particularly fashionable today, try a Sazerac (bourbon and bitters with just a touch of anise) to get a feel for past trends in the

> **Tipping is expected in restaurants— 15–20% of the total bill (before tax).**

city's mixology—it was *de rigeur* at the turn of the last century. Whichever cocktail you like, locally grown or otherwise, you can be sure your talented bartender will mix an excellent example.

If cocktails are not your cup of tea, you will find a full range of American wines and beers, including several local brands brewed in Louisiana. Abita Springs Brewery, 30 miles (48 km) north of New Orleans, produces several brands, including Golden, Amber, Turbo Dog, and Purple Haze. You will also see beers by the Dixie Brewing Company, including their very dark beer, the Blackened Voodoo.

Even coffee isn't ordinary in New Orleans. Louisiana coffee is usually laced with chicory to produce a slightly spicier taste. It is full-flavored and satisfying, often served *au lait* (half hot milk). For an even more exciting finish to a meal, try *café brulot*, hot coffee mixed with spices and liqueurs and flamed over orange peels to produce a warming, intoxicating concoction. If you order coffee in a café, you will normally get refills for free.

You can't say café au lait in New Orleans without saying *beignets* (pronounced bey-nyeys), sweet fried doughnuts without a hole, liberally sprinkled with powdered sugar. You'll always be able to tell who's been eating beignets, because they'll have small smears of sugar on their clothes—and no matter how you try, you'll soon be joining them!

HANDY TRAVEL TIPS

An A–Z Summary of Practical Information

A

ACCOMMODATION

New Orleans offers an extensive range of accommodation, from luxury hotels and historic houses, through slightly more modest hotels, to simple bed-and-breakfast establishments and backpackers' hostels.

The city is unusual in that it has no set high season. Prices of accommodations can vary from week to week depending on whether there are large conventions in town—New Orleans attracts a lot of large conventions—or festivals happening. Always specify any exact dates you have in your itinerary when you inquire about room rates. During the three weeks of Mardi Gras and during the Jazz Festival, New Orleans becomes particularly crowded and accommodation is at a premium. If you intend to visit during this period, you are strongly advised to book accommodation as far in advance as possible.

When room rates are quoted, they may or may not include 9% sales tax plus 2% room tax and a levy of $1 per booked night that supports the work of the New Orleans Convention and Visitors Bureau.

Although the number of B&Bs is growing, many are unregulated. You may feel more confident booking through an agency who can work with you to find an establishment that will meet your needs. Bed and Breakfast Inc. (1021 Moss Street, P.O. Box 52257, New Orleans LA 70152; Tel. (800) 729-4640 (toll-free in US), (504) 488-4640; fax (504) 488-4639) manage a number of historic or interesting properties and will be able to organize special packages for you.

AIRPORT

New Orleans International Airport, also called Moisant International Airport, lies 15 miles (23 km) west of the city. Telephone number for inquiries is (504) 464-0831. There are flights to many major cities throughout the US, and connections to cities worldwide through hub airports of New York, Chicago, Atlanta, and Miami.

Bus services link the airport with the Central Business District in the city at a cost of $1.25. These operate every 15 minutes early in the day (6am–6pm), later every 25 minutes. An airport shuttle runs to the major hotels for $10 per person for a one-way trip; the office is at the arrivals terminal. You'll need to book your return journey with them one day before your departure.

The set taxi fare from or to the airport is $21 for two people, $8 per extra person; the journey time is around 20 minutes.

B

BICYCLE RENTAL/HIRE
The French Quarter is flat with relatively narrow streets, and the journey to the Garden District is also flat all the way—ideal for bike riding. However, there are no cycle lanes or special measures set up to help cyclists, which may present traffic and security difficulties. French Quarter Bicycles at 522 Dumaine Street rents cycles; Tel. (504) 529-3136.

BUDGETING for YOUR TRIP
New Orleans is a relatively inexpensive city to visit, so here are a few guideline prices to help you budget for your trip.

Car rental/hire. Small vehicle per week $120.

VisiTour day pass for bus/trolley car. $5; three day pass $15; single journey $1.25 (you will need exact change).

Entrance fee for Louisiana State Museums. $5 adults, $4 children.

Dinner for one without drinks in a moderate restaurant. $25–35.

Room rate per person per night for a medium room. $130.

Walking tour of the old town. $15.

Horse and buggy tour of the city. $40 for up to 6 people.

Taxi to the airport. $21 for up to 2 people, $8 each additional person.

Swamp tour. $18, or around $35 with transport to the site.

C

CAR RENTAL/HIRE
If you plan to spend your time in the French Quarter, the CBD, and the Garden District, a vehicle will probably be more of a hindrance than a help. The city is compact, which is great for strolling, but

parking is difficult. On-street parking, rules favor residents, and one-way streets can make for some confusion. Parking control staff are extra keen, and cars can be towed for parking violations.

However, if you plan to take trips into the surrounding countryside, touring the plantation route or Cajun country, then it is well worth it to rent. Car rental is relatively inexpensive by international standards, and the condition of the vehicles and customer support is excellent. All the major car-rental companies—Hertz, Avis, and Europcar—have desks at New Orleans airport, so it is possible to pick up a car immediately upon your arrival in the city. Below are the contact details of the major rental companies.

Alamo reservations; Tel. (800) 327-9633 (toll-free in US). Avis nationwide reservations; Tel. (800) 831-2847 (toll-free in US), airport rental station; Tel. (504) 464-9511. Dollar; 1806 Airport Highway; Tel. (504) 467-2285, 230 Loyola Avenue; Tel. (504) 524-1800. Hertz nationwide reservations; Tel. (800) 645-3131 (toll-free in US), New Orleans International Airport; Tel. (504) 468-3695, 901 Convention Boulevard; Tel. (504) 568-1645. National: New Orleans Airport; Tel. (800) 227-7368 (toll-free in US), 324 South Rampart Street; Tel. (504) 525-0416.

Some of the larger rental companies offer more competitive rates if you reserve the car from home.

A small car will cost around $115 per week, medium-sized around $170. All cars have automatic transmission. Insurance covering collision damage and theft will add to these costs (approximately $5 per day), but you may be covered through your domestic vehicle insurance or credit card so make inquiries with them before you sign the rental document.

Many companies have a minimum age limit—usually 21—and you must have held a license for a minimum period of 6 months. Your national license will be acceptable; you will need to show it when you pick up the car. Most rental companies will not allow rental without taking credit card details. If you don't have a credit card, it may be impossible to rent.

CLIMATE

Sultry is a word often used to describe the weather in New Orleans, where the long summers tend to be mercilessly hot and the average rainfall is the highest measured at any US weather station.

The uncomfortably hot season lasts from May to October. At this time take any sightseeing slowly and try to stay out of the sun—most establishments have air-conditioning, which will help a lot. Rain can fall all year but is more likely to arrive in torrential storms between June and November. This is also hurricane season, but warning systems seem to have taken the surprise out of this damaging weather phenomenon, and New Orleans is far enough inland to miss the worst effects of storms that may come ashore in the region.

The most pleasant time of year is usually early spring, Mardi Gras season, when the temperature is warm, not hot, the trees in leaf, and the flowers in full bloom.

For a daily update on weather in the city, call the National Weather Line; Tel. (800) 992-7433 (toll-free in US).

	J	F	M	A	M	J	J	A	S	O	N	D
max °F	62	65	71	77	83	88	90	90	86	79	70	64
°C	17	18	22	25	28	31	32	32	30	26	21	18
min °F	47	50	55	61	68	74	76	76	73	64	55	48
°C	8	10	13	16	20	23	24	24	23	18	13	9

CLOTHING

On hot summer days, T-shirts, light shirts and slacks, or light dresses are ideal. In winter take a light sweater or jacket for chillier days and to wear in the evenings, when it can get cool. Only the smartest restaurants do not allow shorts at lunch.

New Orleans is prone to rain—which comes in heavy downpours—at all times of year. In summer locals set their watches by the afternoon storms, which build with the heat and disperse before sunset. Most people simply find somewhere to shelter during the rain, which floods the streets temporarily and drips from shop awnings and wrought-iron balconies. You may want to carry an umbrella, or take a lightweight raincoat or jacket. If all else fails, many shops sell cheap plastic ponchos to cover your head and clothing.

Comfortable shoes or sandals are a must for strolling the streets of the French Quarter and Garden District.

In the evenings casual attire is acceptable in most establishments, but if you intend to eat at some of the finer restaurants, a jacket for men (ties are rarely required) and a nice ensemble for ladies would be appropriate—make inquiries about dress codes when you make a reservation.

COMPLAINTS

In the first instance complaints should be taken up with the establishment concerned. If you are still dissatisfied, approach either the New Orleans Visitors and Convention Bureau or the Better Business Bureau. They should be able to direct you to the appropriate body, who will advise you further.

CRIME and SAFETY

Where the legacy of the "big easy" is alive and well in terms of great music, fantastic food, and raucous nightlife, so is the crime that has always accompanied it. Until recently New Orleans had a high murder rate compared with other US cities; petty crime rates were also high. New Orleans suburbs are unusual in that the divide between good and not so good neighborhoods is not always obvious—it can be as simple as crossing the street—so you need to be vigilant at all times.

Crime rates have fallen in recent years, and law enforcement has improved greatly—you'll see regular patrols in all the tourist areas. However, crime still exists, and taking a few basic precautions will reduce your chances of becoming a victim. Leave all valuables in your hotel safe, and don't flaunt large amounts of cash or jewelry when you are about town. Don't walk down unlit streets at night. Always take major thoroughfares. Always look confident and informed as you travel around. If you intend to have a few cocktails during your night on the town, take a cab back to our hotel; if you are a little drunk you are more vulnerable to crime. Take a tour if you want to visit the major city cemeteries.

If you visit New Orleans during Mardi Gras, or any other event with large crowds, always be aware of the possibility of pickpockets. Keep cash and credit cards in inside pockets or cash belts. Keep purses closed and, if on a shoulder strap, carry it across your body rather than just over your shoulder.

The Downtown Development District of New Orleans produces a leaflet entitled *New Orleans Street Smart* with safety advice and important telephone numbers in case of emergency.

CUSTOMS and ENTRY REQUIREMENTS

Visas or visa waver: The US operates a visa system for foreign visitors, but there are a number of exceptions. For a number of years it has operated a visa waver scheme for citizens of certain countries, provided that the visitors from those countries have a round-trip ticket and a valid passport. At the present time this includes the UK, Australia, and New Zealand.

Each traveler who is eligible for the visa waver scheme must complete a visa waver form. These will be handed out on the aircraft or at border crossings. The visa waver form will require the address where you will be staying while in the US. The form will be checked by the immigration authorities on entry; you keep the lower portion with you in your passport and relinquish it when you leave the country. You will normally be granted a stay with a 90-day limit, the date will be stamped in your passport.

Canadian citizens will only need proof of residence to enter the United States.

The citizens of all other countries will need a tourist visa for their trip. These can be obtained free of charge from the US Embassy in their respective countries.

Currency restrictions. There are no currency restrictions when entering or leaving the US, but any cash amounts above $10,000 must be declared to US customs on entry or departure.

Customs. Upon arrival, the head of each family must complete a customs declaration form and hand it to the customs official.

Every traveler over the age of 21 may bring in the following items duty free: One liter of wine or hard liquor; 200 cigarettes or 100 cigars (but not Cuban cigars) or 2 lbs of smoking tobacco; $100 worth of gifts. Visitors can enter the US with goods intended for personal use. It is forbidden to carry any foodstuffs or plants into the US and there are stiff penalties for possession of narcotics even in the smallest amounts.

D

DRIVING

If you are bringing your own car, don't forget your driver's license and documents.

Road conditions. Remember to drive on the right. Road conditions are generally good, with traffic controlled by lights at intersections rather than roundabouts (traffic circles). Exits from interstates (motorways) can be from the left lane or the right, especially in the downtown city center area. Always be aware of which side the exit is on. Passing is allowed on either side of a vehicle on an interstate or multiple-lane road.

Rules and regulations. Drivers and front-seat passengers must use seat belts; rear-seat passengers must also use seat belts if they are available. Motorcycle riders must wear a helmet.

Under Louisiana law the speed limit on urban interstate highways is 70 mph (112 km/h). On other highways, including urban areas, it varies from 30 mph (48 km/h) upwards. These speed limits can vary within local county (parish) limits, and can even change several times on the same stretch of road, so always keep alert for speed limit changes. The prevailing speed limit is posted on round signs at the roadside. School zones have a speed limit of 20 mph (32 km/h). This is applicable when lights are flashing on the "school zone" signs. If you are following a school bus (bright yellow vehicle) with its lights flashing, do not pass when it stops to let pupils alight. You must stop behind the bus until it moves on.

New Orleans

Turning right on a red light is legal in Louisiana unless prohibited by a notice at the light. Always be aware of both pedestrian and vehicular traffic if you turn right on a red light.

Fuel costs. Gasoline is inexpensive in the US—approximately $1.50 per gallon for premium grade. Most garages have self-service pumps, all of which give measurements in gallons. You will find stations in all major towns and most will have a 24-hour pump that dispenses gas automatically with payment by credit card. Many gas stations will expect you to pre-pay for gas, especially after dark.

Parking. You can park on the street provided there are no restrictions, but in reality street parking is a problem; many streets will have sections for resident parking with fines and towing for those who break the rules. Street parking is expensive, generally over $1.50 per hour. You'll need plenty of change for the meters. There are parking lots throughout the city, but they fill up quickly. Some hotels have private parking areas—even a few in the French Quarter. Ask about facilities and any extra charges before you make a firm reservation if parking is important for you.

If you need help. Most rental cars come with coverage from a reputable recovery or breakdown service. The American Automobile Association (AAA) offers breakdown service and other advice to motorists in the USA. You may be entitled to help from them at no extra charge through your domestic vehicle coverage with a breakdown company. Make inquiries before you travel, or contact AAA at Tel. (800) 222-4357 (toll-free in the US) for coverage within the US.

Road signs. The US has a number of symbols which are readily understandable by most English visitors. The following written signs may be confusing:

American	*British*
Roadway	Carriageway
No parking by highway	Clearway

Detour	Diversion
Divided highway	Dual carriageway
Yield	Give way
Railroad crossing	Level crossing
Expressway	Motorway
No passing	No overtaking
Men working	Roadworks
Traffic circle	Roundabout

In New Orleans, especially in the French Quarter and the CBD, you will find one-way streets to prevent bottlenecks. If you intend to drive around the city it would help to invest in a good map to aid navigation.

Fluid measures

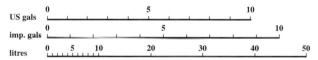

Distance

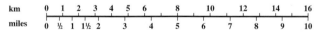

E

ELECTRICITY

The standard current in the US is 110 volt, 60 cycle AC. All visitors except Canadians will need a transformer and adapter for their electric appliances. Adapters are available at airport shops. Most hotels have special sockets for shavers and hairdryers that operate on 240 or 110 volts.

EMBASSIES and CONSULATES

Most countries' consular and embassy services operate through Washington DC, the capital of the US.

Australia: (*embassy*) 1601 Massachusetts Avenue NW, Washington DC 20036; Tel. (202) 797-3000; web site <www.austemb.org>

Canada: (*embassy*) 501 Pennsylvania Avenue NW, Washington DC 20001; Tel. (202) 682-1740; web site <www.cdnemb-washdc.org>

New Zealand: (*embassy*) 37 Observatory Circle NW, Washington DC 20008; Tel. (202) 328-4800; web site <www.emb.com/nzemb>

Republic of Ireland: (*embassy*) 2234 Massachusetts Avenue NW, Washington DC 20008; Tel. (202) 462-3939

South Africa: (*embassy*) 3051 Massachusetts Avenue NW, Washington DC 20008; Tel. (202) 232-4400.

UK: (*embassy*) 3100 Massachusetts Avenue NW, Washington DC 20008; Tel. (202) 462-1340

EMERGENCIES

The emergency telephone number is the same throughout the entire US. Dial 911 and you will be connected to an operator who will ask you the nature of the emergency. The operator will then be able to summon police, firefighters, ambulance (medical aid), or all three services, depending on the nature of the emergency. This is a free call from pay phones. It would be helpful to have as many details as possible about your location when you ring the emergency services in order for them to reach you quickly.

G

GAY and LESBIAN TRAVELERS

New Orleans is a very gay-friendly destination, with a high concentration of gay inhabitants, bars, and hotels, along with many established local businesses and services. The Gay and Lesbian Community Center can be found at 2114 Decatur Street; Tel. (504) 945-1103. *Ambush Mag*, aimed at the gay and lesbian community, is published weekly; they also have a web site at <www.ambushmag.

com>. You could also start with <www.gayneworleans.com>, which offers useful information and links to other sites.

GETTING THERE

By Air

More than a dozen airlines fly into Moisant International in New Orleans. The major ones are: American Airlines; Tel. (800) 433-7300 (toll-free in US); web site <www.aa.com>, Continental; Tel. (800) 525-0280 (toll-free in US); web site <www.flycontinetal.com>, Delta; Tel. (800) 221-1212 (toll-free in US); web site <www.delta-air.com>, and US Airways; Tel. (800) 428-4322 (toll-free in US); web site <www.usairways.com>.

Air Canada flies from various cities; Tel. (800) 776-3000 (toll-free in Canada).

No airlines have international flights direct to New Orleans from Europe, Australia, New Zealand, South Africa, or the UK. The following airlines operate international connections into the US for onward flights to New Orleans: Delta has flights from the UK via Atlanta and reciprocal agreements with South African Airlines for routes from South Africa into the US. British Airways (Tel. 0181/759 5511; web site <www.british-airways.com>) has numerous routes to the US, as does American Airlines, through a major hub in Chicago. Virgin offers transatlantic flights from the UK via New York, Newark, and Miami; Tel. (01293) 747-747.

From the Republic of Ireland, Aer Lingus offers direct flights to New York with connections through American carriers to New Orleans; Tel. (01) 844-4777.

From Australia and New Zealand, several companies offer a trip across the Pacific: Quantas (Tel. (008) 112-121, toll-free in Sydney) and Air New Zealand (Tel. (09) 357-3000) fly to Los Angeles with onward connection through an American carrier.

By Car

You can reach New Orleans along major route I10 from the east or west, plus I55, US90 or US61. For comparison, New Orleans is 6 hours driving time from Memphis, Tennessee, 7 hours from Houston, Texas, and 6 hours from Jacksonville, Florida.

The I10 cuts a path through the city — take the Poydras exit for the CDB and Vieux Carré for the French Quarter. It would be advisable to have directions to your hotel to avoid finding yourself in the wrong neighborhood.

By Train
Amtrak offers services that terminate at Union Passenger Terminal, 1001 Loyola Avenue, in the CBD. For prices and schedules, including information on rail passes if you intend to visit other places in the US; Tel. (800) USA-RAIL (toll-free in US), or (504) 526-1610.

By Bus
Greyhound Trailways offers a comprehensive network of coach/bus services throughout the US, including a regular service to the Union Passenger Terminal at 1001 Loyola Avenue in the CBD. For details on the schedules; Tel. (800) 231-2222 (toll-free in US), or (504) 524-7571.

GUIDES and TOURS
There are a number of different kinds of tours for those exploring the New Orleans region.

Themed walking tours are a great favorite; you can take tours of the French Quarter that offer a simple historic narrative, or architectural tours, ghost tours, and even bordello tours. Tours are available in the day and evening; here are some of the options available:

New Orleans Historic Walking Tours (see page 89): contact them at Historic Walking Tours Inc., P.O. Box 19381, New Orleans, LA 70179; Tel. (504) 947-2120; fax (504) 947-2130; web site <www.tourneworleans.com>. No credit card payments.

Friends of the Cabildo (see page 89). No booking is necessary; arrive at 523 St. Ann Street at 1:20pm. Adults 21 and over $10, seniors and children under 13–21 $8; Tel. (504) 523-3939; web site <www.gnofn.org/~fcabildo>.

If you want to tour the French Quarter without walking, take a horse-and-buggy ride. All the carriage-drivers are knowledgeable about the city and have amusing stories to tell about its past inhabitants. Find the carriages at the river side of Jackson Square.

Grey Line offer a number of coach tours, including a city tour, plus plantation tours with pick-up at city center locations; Tel. 800-535-7786 (toll-free in the US); (504) 569-1401.

H

HEALTH and MEDICAL CARE

There are no serious health concerns to worry about when you visit New Orleans. Minor concerns include over imbibing and overeating, so it may be advisable to have antacid tablets and aspirin— or to pace your intake. Mosquitoes can be a problem, especially out in the countryside. Always carry insect repellent and apply it regularly. Louisiana does have some species of venomous snake and spider. When out in the countryside don't walk off the beaten track, and avoid probing dense undergrowth or piles of leaves. Be aware of crocodiles if you travel in the bayous; they can move with great speed

Unless you have recently visited a yellow fever or other epidemic area, you will not need any inoculations to enter the US.

It is safe to drink the tap water in New Orleans.

There is no free medical treatment available in the US, even for emergency situations. Just a trip in an ambulance can be expensive, running into several hundreds of dollars, so insurance is vital for your trip. Having proof of adequate insurance will smooth the process if you do need treatment, though not having insurance does not mean that you will not be treated—simply that you will be faced with a bill which will have to be paid.

A number of hospitals offer emergency treatment facilities in the city. The nearest one to the French Quarter is University Hospital on Perdido Street. 24-hour emergency telephone number; Tel. (504) 588-3144.

A range of over-the-counter drugs are available for everyday ailments; pharmacists will be able to advise you on minor ailments.

HITCHHIKING

Hitchhiking is not illegal in the US. Walking with thumb raised toward the road is a sign that you are looking for a lift. However, this is a particularly unsafe mode of transportation. All usual safety warnings apply; females traveling alone are more vulnerable.

HOLIDAYS

The following dates are public holidays. This does not mean that shops and restaurants will be closed, but offices and banks will be. Where a holiday falls on a Saturday or Sunday, the following Monday will be taken as the official holiday.

1 January	*New Year's Day*
3rd Monday in January	*Martin Luther King, Jr. Day*
3rd Monday in February	*President's Day*
Last Monday in May	*Memorial Day*
4 July	*Independence Day*
1st Monday in September	*Labor Day*
2nd Monday in October	*Columbus Day*
11 November	*Veterans Day*
4th Thursday in November	*Thanksgiving*
25 December	*Christmas Day*

Although not an official holiday, most businesses in New Orleans also close on Mardi Gras Day.

LANGUAGE

The US has English as a first language, though many words used are different to UK or other forms of English. The Cajun community in southern Louisiana speaks French with an ancient sentence construction and vocabulary, though most Cajuns also speak English.

LAUNDRY and DRY CLEANING

There are numerous self-service laundries in the French Quarter and business districts near the major hotels. Below are several that will pick up your laundry, wash, dry, and fold or dry-clean your clothes. You can drop off or they will pick up and deliver.

Hula Mae's, 840 North Rampart Street; Tel. (504) 522-1336

Washing Well Laundryteria, 841 Bourbon Street; Tel. (504) 523-9955

M

MAPS

A number of tourist maps of the city can be found in tourist information centers. These will be adequate for sightseeing, particularly on foot in the French Quarter, CBD, and the Garden District.

For travel in Louisiana, the Department of Transportation and Development produces an official highway map for free distribution. Contact them at P.O. Box 94245 Capitol Station, Baton Rouge, LA 70804.

MEDIA

Newspapers. The main daily New Orleans newspaper for interesting, up-to-the-minute information is *The Times-Picayune*. An extra arts information section on Fridays called *Lagniappe* will tell you what's happening around the city in the week ahead.

Offbeat is a free monthly magazine that focuses on arts entertainment. You will find it in hotels, some cafés, and at visitor information centers. *Gambit Weekly* is a free magazine covering all the arts, reviewing galleries, interior design, and new performances in dance, theatre, music, and cinema. It has interesting articles as well as performance listings.

All the major US newspapers are readily available at newsstands; many hotels will have copies in the reception area.

Television. Most hotels in the city will offer a news channel such as CNN as part of their media service. The local news channels serving the city are WWL (CBS, channel 4), WDSU (NBC, channel 6), and WVUE (ABC, channel 8).

MONEY

The official currency of the US is the dollar ($). Notes are printed in $1, $5, $10, $20, $50, and $100. Each dollar is made up of 100 cents; coins are found in denominations of 1¢ (penny), 5¢ (nickel), 10¢ (dime), 25¢ (quarter), and the rarer 50¢ (half dollar) and $1 coins.

Currency exchange. Banks are open Monday–Friday 9am–3pm, but changing foreign currency is not a regular activity for them; it can be a time-consuming business. It will help to bring some dollars with you, and to carry traveler's checks in dollars (see below).

ATMs. Most banks, shopping malls, and many hotels and bars have ATMs that accept international debit cards—look for the Cirrus or Plus signs on the ATM. If you have trouble locating a machine, call Cirrus (Tel. 800/424-7787, toll-free in US) or Plus (Tel. 800/843-7587, toll-free in US) for information on the ATM nearest you. Most machines will also dispense cash against major credit cards. Some machines will impose an extra charge on withdrawals on out-of-state or foreign banks. Always be aware of your surroundings and security if you obtain money at a bar or a store.

Credit cards. The US loves its credit cards, and hotels will normally ask for an imprint for incidentals. It will be almost impossible to rent a vehicle without one. They are also widely accepted for payment in hotels, restaurants, and shops, reducing the need to carry cash in large quantities.

Traveler's checks. Most hotels and many major stores are happy to accept travelers checks in payment. Do get them in US dollars, as any other currency is more difficult to exchange. You can also cash traveler's checks at banks and hotels.

OPEN HOURS

Banks are open Monday through Friday 9am–3pm, though most have ATMs for 24-hour cash withdrawals (not all offer international withdrawal facilities from your checking or current account, so look for the Plus or Cirrus signs).

Offices are generally open Monday–Friday, 9am–5pm.

Post offices are open Monday–Friday 9am–5:30pm, Saturday 9am–12:30pm.

Shops are generally open Monday–Saturday, 9am–6:30pm; Sunday 11am–5pm. They may stay open until 8 or 9pm in the French Quarter. Major malls also remain open until 9pm.

Restaurants generally open from 12pm–3pm and 6pm–10pm, these hours may vary, especially during Mardi Gras. Restaurants will often close on Mondays.

Most attractions are open 9am–5pm daily, though state museums are closed on Mondays.

POLICE

If you need the police, find a telephone box and dial 911. You will be connected to an operator who will put you in touch with the emergency service you need.

The blue-uniformed police are armed; in central New Orleans/the French Quarter you will find them on foot and horse patrols along with the motorcycle and vehicle patrols that prevail in the suburbs. They are extremely courteous and helpful to visitors.

The headquarters of the New Orleans Police Department in the French Quarter is at 334 Royal Street; Tel. (504) 565-7530. There is also an office at 501 North Rampart Street; Tel. (504) 565-7500.

The Downtown Development District of New Orleans prints a leaflet entitled *New Orleans Street Smart,* with safety advice and important telephone numbers in case of emergency.

POST OFFICES

The US Postal Service deals with postage only. It offers reasonable service, with postcards to Europe arriving in 3–5 days. The main post office in the CBD is at 701 Loyola Avenue, but many postcard shops and drugstores sell stamps, and most hotels will post cards for you. Mailing a postcard within the US costs 20¢; overseas 55¢.

PUBLIC TRANSPORTATION

Buses and trolleys. New Orleans has a good public transportation system that will take you to most of the major attractions efficiently and cheaply. The St. Charles streetcar runs from Canal Street through the CBD, then skirts the Warehouse District and the Garden District before traveling to the universities and Audubon Park and Zoo, terminating at Carrolton. It runs every 15 minutes between 7am and 7pm, less frequently after that, 24 hours a day. The Riverfront trolley runs from the downriver end of French Market (at the Old US Mint) to Riverwalk. This trolley car has ramp access.

Bus number 11 runs from Canal Street along the whole length of Magazine Street to Audubon Park and Zoo. The Esplanade bus runs along North Rampart Street and up Esplanade Avenue to City Park. It runs at 30-minute intervals.

A one-day VisiTour ticket costs $5, three-day $12. Single journeys throughout the city cost $1.25 per person—if you want to transfer from trolley or bus to another trolley or bus, it costs an extra 25¢ per person. Exact change is required.

Information on all routes can be obtained from the Regional Transit Authority (RTA); Tel. (504) 827-RIDE (7433).

Ferry. The Canal Street ferry, which plies a route across the Mississippi to Algiers twice each hour, is free for foot passengers.

Taxis. Taxis offer good service in the city. You can hail them on the street or stand in taxi lines at major hotels. Rates start at $2.10 minimum, with 75¢ extra for each passenger after the first. A small charge is added for more than two bags per person. Each 30-second time interval adds 30¢. Taxis can be rented for $22 per hour, with extra charges for more bodies to a maximum of $55 per hour. This could be a good option for touring outside the city if you don't want to drive.

Horse-drawn buggies. These offer tours rather than journeys. For $40 (up to 6 people), they will carry you through the French Quarter with informative commentary on all the major historic buildings and incidents.

RELIGION
New Orleans is a predominantly Roman Catholic city but there are Protestant churches—Baptist, Episcopal, Lutheran, Methodist, Presbyterian—and most other major religions are represented. Hotel concierges have lists of addresses and times of services.

TELEPHONE
The city code for New Orleans is 504. When making an international call always dial 00 before the country code; the country code for the US from other countries is 1.

International codes from the United States are as follows:

Australia	61	Canada	1
Ireland	353	New Zealand	64
South Africa	27	United Kingdom	44

Most hotels will offer direct-dial long distance and international phone facilities, but these can be extremely expensive. A more cost-effective solution is to use a pre-paid calling card (available from drugstores around the city; simply follow the instructions on the back of the card) or calling company who will charge your call to your credit card. Look for information on long-distance providers in your hotel room; many will give contact details and instructions for making a connection from your room phone. Alternatively, ask hotel reception if they offer one.

Phone calls can be make from phone booths and kiosks using coins, credit cards, and calling cards, although older booths may only accept coins. Phone cards of various denominations can be purchased from newsagents, post offices, tourist information offices, and drug stores.

TICKETS

There is no central ticket agency for tickets to sporting, festival, or arts events in the city. The New Orleans Visitors and Convention Center can provide individual numbers for each event; Tel. (800) 672-6124 (toll-free in US), (504) 566-5011; fax (504) 566-5046; web site <www.neworleanscvb.com>.

Jazz Festival tickets can be obtained be mail from Ticketmaster; Tel. (800) 488-5252 (toll free in US), (504) 522-5555. Have your credit card ready.

TIME ZONES

New Orleans is in the Central time zone, which is 1 hour behind Eastern Standard Time.

Los Angeles	**New Orleans**	New York	London	Sydney
10am	**noon**	1pm	6pm	3am (next day)

TIPPING

In the US, it is almost always the customer's responsibility to pay for the service received. In restaurants, this means a tip of 15–20% of the total bill.

Bus boys	$1 per bag
Cleaning staff	$5 for short stays, $1 per day for longer stays
Taxi drivers	about 15%
Bar staff	small change from each round of drinks
Hairdresser/barber	15%
Hotel maid	$1 per day (except for very short stays)

TOILETS

There are clean and tidy public toilets at the following locations; ask for the "rest room": Canalside and Riverwalk Malls; French Market; below Washington Artillery Battery; City Park.

There may be a small charge for the use of some facilities. Most tourist attractions also have public toilet facilities.

TOURIST INFORMATION

The main Visitor Information Center for the city can be found at 529 St. Ann, on the downriver side of Jackson Square; Tel. (504) 566-5031. This office is open 9am–5pm and has maps, hotel information, and tour information.

There is also an office at Moisant Airport if you want to gather information immediately upon your arrival; Tel. (504) 464-0831.

If you require information about New Orleans before you travel, contact the New Orleans Metropolitan Convention and Visitors Bureau (NOMAVB) at 1520 Sugar Bowl Drive, New Orleans, Louisiana 70112; Tel. (800) 672-6124 (toll-free in US) or (504) 566 5055; web site <www.nawlins.com>. They have up-to-date and comprehensive publications covering all aspects of a visit to the Big Easy.

The Louisiana State Office of Culture, Recreation, and Tourism can provide information about activities within the state—Mississippi River Road, Cajun Country, etc. For further information, contact them at 1051 North Third Street, Baton Rouge, LA 70802; Tel. (800) 395-1939 (toll-free in US) or (504) 342-8100; web site <www.louisianatravel.com>.

WEB SITES

Web sites can be found in the contact details of individual attractions, hotels, and restaurants throughout this guide, but here are a few others that may help you plan your trip.

<www.neworleansweb.org>

<www.gayneworleans.com>

New Orleans

<www.gumbopages.com>

<www.insideneworleans.com> from Cox communications.

<www.neworleansonline.com>

<www.nolalive.com> from the *Times Picayune*.

<www.nojazzfest.com> the official Jazz Festival web site.

<www.frenchquarter.com> concentrating on the Vieux Carré area.

WEIGHTS and MEASURES

The conversion in the US to metric weights and measures is still set to take place, but in most everyday situations you will still find imperial measurements used—inches, feet, yards, miles, ounces, pounds, pints, and gallons.

Length

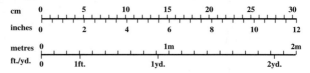

Weight

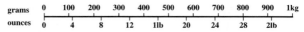

Temperature

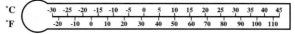

YOUTH HOSTELS

There are a number of YMCA hotels around the city. The main site is in the warehouse district on Lee Circle, 920 Charles Avenue; Tel. (504) 568-9622.

Recommended Hotels

New Orleans offers a great deal of accommodation — from huge, 5-star hotels to intimate bed-and-breakfasts — with price ranges to match. But even with this large number of rooms it can be difficult to find a vacancy. It is important to book well in advance if you plan to stay during one of the city's major festivals: Mardi Gras (usually in February) and the Jazz and Heritage Festival (late April–early May) are the biggest. And as New Orleans hosts many conventions, rooms can be almost nonexistent for no reason readily apparent to the visitor if there are a few big conventions in town. Being flexible may help you find a better bargain, so try to plan around a given time rather than an exact date.

If you wish to contact the following hotels by telephone from outside the US, dial 001 before the local area code (504) and telephone number.

The following price range indicates the price of a double room per night. There is generally no set high season, but prices change dramatically throughout the year: they are generally much higher for the major festivals.

$$$$$	over $250
$$$$	$175–250
$$$	$140–175
$$	$90–140
$	under $90

French Quarter

Cornstalk Hotel $$$ *915 Royal Street, New Orleans 70140; Tel. (504) 523-1515*. This French Quarter landmark house with its wrought-iron fence is a must-see on the walking tour. Typical Victorian architecture and antique furniture are as pretty as you would expect—there's nothing else like it in the Quarter, and the location is superb. Though the house has its eccentricities, this will add to the charm for some. Rooms are different sizes, so ask when booking. 14 rooms. Major credit cards.

Hotel Maison de Ville and Audubon Cottages $$$$
727 Toulouse Street (cottages 535-725), New Orleans 70130; Tel. (800) 634-1600 (toll-free in US), (504) 561-5858; fax (504) 528-9939; web site <www.maisondeville.com>. This pretty courtyard hotel is a real find. Tennessee Williams stayed here regularly. Antiques and feather cushions abound. Individually styled rooms vary greatly in size. Facilities include outdoor pool, room service, valet parking, complimentary port in the afternoon. 23 rooms. Major credit cards.

Landmark French Quarter $$–$$$ *920 Rampart Street, New Orleans 70116; Tel. (800) 535-7860 (toll-free in US and Canada); 0-800-891-383 (toll-free in UK), (504) 524-3333; fax (504) 522-8044*. On the edge of the French Quarter with rooms facing onto a pleasant courtyard. Rooms offer satellite TV, ceiling fan, coffee, safe. Pool, bar, restaurant, coin laundry, shuttle service to riverfront, car park (extra charge). 100 rooms. Major credit cards.

Le Richelieu $$–$$$ *1234 Rue Chartres, New Orleans 70116; Tel. (800) 535-9653 (toll-free in US and Canada), (504) 529-2492; fax (504) 524-8179*. One of the friendliest hotels in the French Quarter, the Richelieu has had many celebrity guests. It's at the quieter, downriver end of town, across the street from Faubourg Marigny and its nightlife. Rooms have satellite TV, telephone, mini-bar. Facilities include bar, pool, and free parking. 69 rooms. Major credit cards.

The Maison Dupuy $$$$ *1001 Rue Toulouse, New Orleans 70112; Tel. (800) 535-9177 (toll-free in US and Canada), (504)*

586-8000; fax (504) 525-5334. Five beautifully renovated town houses make up the Maison Dupuy. Situated on the edge of the French Quarter, it's a short stroll from all the action but away from the hubbub. A fine hotel, yet small enough to be intimate and cozy. The elegant rooms feature iron/ironing boards, hairdryers, TV, telephones with data-ports. Full size pool, fitness room, Jacuzzi, bar, and Dominique's restaurant. Valet parking $16 per day. 200 rooms. Major credit cards.

The Monteleone $$$–$$$$ *214 Royal Street, New Orleans 70130; Tel. (800) 535-9595 (toll-free in US), (504) 523-3341; fax (504) 528-1019; web site <www.hotelmonteleone.com>*. One of the oldest large hotels in the French Quarter, the Monteleone is still family-owned. Beautiful public areas are its trademark. Rooms are either furnished with antiques or in a more modern style, and include satellite TV, telephone. Facilities include pool, fitness room, sauna, restaurant, room service. Valet parking. Wheelchair access. 597 rooms. Major credit cards.

Omni Royal Orleans Hotel $$$–$$$$ *621 St. Louis Street, New Orleans 70140; Tel. (800) THE-OMNI (toll-free in US), (504) 529-5333; fax (504) 529-7089; web site <www.omnihotels.com>*. The Omni sits almost in the heart of the French Quarter, next to the Law Courts. Rooms have satellite TV, telephone, mini-bar, iron/ironing board. Facilities include pool, fitness room, Rib Room restaurant, 24-hour room service. Parking. Wheelchair access. 346 rooms. Major credit cards.

Royal Sonesta Hotel $$$$–$$$$$ *300 Bourbon Street, New Orleans 70140; Tel. (800) 766-3782 (toll-free in US), (504) 586-0300; fax (504) 586-0335; web site <www.royalsonestano. com>*. Situated in the heart of the Bourbon Street action, the Royal Sonesta offers a quiet, luxury escape from the raucous behavior outside. Rooms have satellite TV, telephone, mini-bar, robes, hairdryer. Facilities include pool, restaurant, fitness room, room service. Valet parking. Wheelchair access. 485 rooms. Major credit cards.

The Frenchmen Hotel $–$$$$ *417 Frenchmen Street, New Orleans 70116; Tel. (800) 831-1781 (toll-free in US), (504) 948-2166; fax (504) 948-2258;* This small, individual hotel is not for everyone (it has been described as "funky") but it's great for someone looking for an experience. It sits at the edge of the French Quarter and the Faubourg Marigny—great for nightlife, yet only a stroll away from places of interest. The hotel comprises two 19th-century houses so rooms vary in size; antique furniture predominates. Rooms have TV. Facilities include pool. Free parking. 28 rooms. Major credit cards.

Greater New Orleans

Grand Boutique $$$$ *2001 St. Charles Avenue, New Orleans 70130; Tel. (504) 558-9966; fax (504) 571-6464.* Directly on the St. Charles Streetcar line, this hotel became the center of a furor when it opened. Its 1890 skeleton has been dressed in Art Deco style, much to the consternation of author Anne Rice, who was very vocal in her opposition. The décor is different from anything else available in the city. Rooms are large, each with spa bath, fridge, microwave, coffee, telephone, safe, data-port, and satellite TV. Wheelchair access. Parking. 44 rooms. Major credit cards.

Hyatt Regency New Orleans $$–$$$$ *500 Poydras Plaza, New Orleans 70113; Tel. (800) 233-1234 (toll-free in US), (504) 561-1234; fax (504) 552-4210; web site <www.hyatt.com>.* This huge hotel serves many of the conventions which hit town each year, but it still provides a good standard of accommodation—though it is a bit impersonal due to its size. Next to the Superdome; short taxi ride to the French Quarter/Riverwalk—free shuttle provided.

Rooms have satellite TV, coffee, mini-bar, telephone. Facilities include pool, restaurant, fitness room. Valet parking. Wheelchair access. 1184 rooms. Major credit cards.

Hilton New Orleans Riverside $$$$–$$$$$ *2 Poydras Street, New Orleans 70140; Tel. (800) 445-8667 (toll-free in US), (504) 561-0500; fax (504) 568-1721; web site <www.hilton. com>.* Situated on the riverfront with interior connection to Riverwalk mall, this hotel is perfect for bad-weather stays—with easy access to cinemas, Harrah's casino, and the Aquarium. Pete Fountain performs at his club here. Rooms have satellite TV, mini-bar. Facilities include pool, restaurant, fitness room, 24-hour room service, eligibility for pass to Rivercentre Leisure Center. Parking. Wheelchair access. 1600 rooms. Major credit cards.

Hotel Inter-continental $$$–$$$$ *444 Charles Avenue, New Orleans 70130; Tel. (800) 445-6563 (toll-free in US), (504) 525-5566; fax (504) 585-4350; web site <www. interconti.com>.* Recently refurbished, with newly decorated and furnished rooms, the Inter-continental often caters to convention and business visitors. It is well situated for the independent traveler, however; on the streetcar route and a short stroll to the French Quarter. Rooms have satellite TV, telephone, mini-bar. Facilities include pool, restaurant, fitness room, 24-hour room service. Valet parking. Wheelchair access. 482 rooms. Major credit cards.

International House Hotel $$–$$$$ *221 Camp Street, New Orleans 70130; Tel. (800) 633-5770 (toll-free in US), (504) 200-5605; fax (504) 200-6532; web site <www.ihhotel.com>.* One of the newer hotels in town, International House sets the standard in design and style, offering something unique to the city. Rooms are modern yet retro, with TV with movie channels, CD player with range of music, hairdryer, data-ports, telephone.

Facilities include restaurant, fitness room. Parking. Wheelchair access. Rates include breakfast. 116 rooms. Major credit cards.

Le Meridien $$$–$$$$ *614 Canal Street, New Orleans 70130; Tel. (800) 543-4300 (toll-free in US), (504) 525-6500; fax (504) 586-1543; web site <www.meridienneworleans.com>.* Situated just outside the French Quarter, within easy reach of the St. Charles streetcar. Rooms have modem access, voicemail, coffee, satellite TV, hairdryer. Facilities include restaurant, heated rooftop pool, health club, sauna, 24-hour room service, gift shops. Wheelchair access. Parking. 494 rooms. Major credit cards.

Le Pavillon Hotel $$–$$$$ *833 Poydras Street, New Orleans 70112; Tel. (800) 535-9095 (toll-free in US), (504) 581-3111; fax (504) 522-5543; web site <www.lepavillon.com>.* This very striking hotel, with a columned entrance reminiscent of a Classical Greek temple, was opened in 1907. The public rooms are stunning. Located on the main street of the CBD a short stroll from the waterfront and French Quarter. Facilities include pool, fitness room, spa, restaurant, 24-hour room service, complimentary hors d'oeuvres 4pm–7pm. Rooms have minibar, microwave, satellite TV, telephone. Wheelchair access. Parking. 226 rooms. Major credit cards.

St. Charles Inn $–$$ *3636 St. Charles Avenue, New Orleans 70115; Tel. (800) 489-9908 (toll-free in US), (504) 899-8888; fax (504) 899-8892.* This popular budget option sits on the St. Charles Streetcar route with easy access to downtown. Rooms are modest, but have satellite TV and telephone. Facilities include restaurant. Rates include breakfast. Wheelchair accessible. Free parking. 40 rooms. Major credit cards.

Wyndham Canal Place $$$$ *100 Rue Iberville, New Orleans 70130; Tel. (504) 566-7006; fax (504) 553-5120; web site*

<www.wyndham.com>. Large, modern luxury hotel perfectly situated on the banks of the river, above Canal Place Shopping Mall. Rooms have satellite TV, coffee, mini-bar, telephone. Facilities include pool, fitness room, spa, restaurant. Wheelchair access. Parking. 438 rooms. Major credit cards.

Windsor Court Hotel $$$$$ *300 Gravier Street, New Orleans 70130; Tel. (800) 262-2662 (toll-free in US), (504) 523-6000; fax (504) 596-4513*. This hotel has been voted the best in North America by a reputable travel magazine. Fine antiques fill this refuge from the outside world; the whole building has an up-market and luxurious feel. Suites only, with satellite TV, telephone with data-port, robes. Facilities include pool, restaurant, health club, kitchenettes, in-room massage. Wheelchair access. Parking. 324 rooms. Major credit cards.

Louisiana

Madewod Plantation House $$$$ *4250 Highway 308, Napoleonville 70390; Tel. (800) 375-7151 (toll-free in US); fax (504) 369-7151; web site <www.madewood.com>*. Historic ante-bellum mansion offering genteel surroundings and friendly service. Some rooms set in cottages in the grounds; all are furnished with antiques. Room rate also includes dinner. 8 rooms. Major credit cards.

Maison des Amis/Chez des Amis $–$$$ *140 East Bridge Street, Breaux Bridge 70517; Tel. (318) 332-5273; fax (318) 332-2227; web site <www.cafedesamis.com>*. Award-winning, restored Creole cottages furnished in unique style—some modern, some antique. Maison des Amis sits beside the bayou in a garden with gazebo. Breakfasts taken at Café des Amis. Complimentary beverages, communal microwave. Two rooms are not en-suite —ask when booking. Wheelchair access. Parking. 6 rooms. Major credit cards.

Recommended Restaurants

Eating out is one of the highlights of a trip to New Orleans. With a very particular cuisine and superb standards set by a few families in the early days, those who have opened restaurants in recent years have had little option but to operate at the same level as the old firms.

The mainstay of the city is Creole and Cajun, but you'll find a range of other cuisines on offer. There's no chance of becoming jaded with the good sushi, Italian, Thai, and fast food available. Just remember to bring your appetite, because portions are large!

Reservations are always required at the best establishments, especially when there's a lot going on in the city (see page TK for dates of major festivals) Don't forget to ask about the dress code; a jacket is usually required for men in the evenings. If you're not from the US, remember that restaurants close relatively early (usually 10pm) here, so don't go out for dinner too late.

If you wish to make reservations from outside the US, dial 001 before the local area code (504) and telephone number.

The following price ranges indicate the cost of a three-course dinner for one person without drinks.

$$$$$	over $50
$$$$	$35–50
$$$	$25–35
$$	$15–25
$	under $15

French Quarter

Acme Oyster House $ *724 Iberville, New Orleans 70130; Tel. (800) 994-2006 (toll-free in the US), (504) 522-5973; fax*

(504) 524-1595. The best oyster house in the French Quarter; you can drop in throughout the day to eat a few with a cold beer. Great Po-boys too. The place is loud and busy, so it's not optimal for a romantic meal. Open Monday–Saturday 11am–10pm, Sunday noon–7pm. Major credit cards.

Arnaud's $$$$ *813 Bienville, New Orleans 70112; Tel. (504) 523-5433; web site <www.arnauds.com>*. One of the signature restaurants of the French Quarter. The main dining room at Arnaud's, with its wood, tile, and glass, could have been spirited directly from an avenue in Paris. The service is attentive and the French/Creole food superb. On the premises, a Mardi Gras Museum features personal memorabilia and costumes from the family of the founder of Arnaud's. Open daily: lunch Monday–Friday 11am–2:30pm, brunch and jazz Saturday–Sunday 10am–2:30pm, dinner 6pm–10pm. Reservations recommended. Jacket required at dinner. Validated parking. Major credit cards.

BACCO $$$ *310 Chartres Street, New Orleans 70130; Tel. (504) 522-2426; fax (504) 521-8323; web site <www.bacco. com>*. Beautiful, modern restaurant from the Brennan stables serving classical Italian cuisine. Wonderful fresh ingredients in complex dishes. The menu changes regularly but is always good. Elegant surroundings. Open lunch Monday–Saturday 11:30am–2:30pm, Sunday brunch 10am–2pm, dinner daily 6pm–10pm. Major credit cards.

Brennan's Restaurant $$$$ *417 Rue Royale, New Orleans 70130; Tel. (504) 525-9711; fax (504) 525-2302*. Famed for its breakfast and brunch, Brennan's is a must-do on a trip to New Orleans. The Brennan family invented Bananas Foster, so try it after a generous entrée accompanied by wines from their excellent list—yes, with breakfast! Eggs any way, steak, and veal are all available and beautifully presented. Open daily: breakfast/brunch 8am–2:30pm, lunch 11:30am–2:30pm weekdays only, dinner 6pm–10pm. Reservations recommended. Jacket required at dinner. Validated parking with dinner reservations. Major credit cards.

Café du Monde $ *800 Decatur Street, New Orleans 70116; Tel. (800) 772-2927 (toll-free in US), (504) 587-0883; fax (504) 587-0847; web site <www.cafedumonde.com>. The* place in New Orleans for *café au lait* and *beignets*, though it gets a little sticky with powdered sugar on breezy days (examine your seat before you sit down). Everyone comes here — including locals — to sit and watch the world go by. Open 24 hours a day, seven days a week. Cash only.

The Court of Two Sisters $$$$ *613 Rue Royale, New Orleans 70130; Tel. (504) 522-7261; fax (504) 581-5804; web site <www.courtoftwosisters.com>*. Set in a large open courtyard (weather permitting) or in the dining room, the jazz buffet brunch features over 40 hot and cold dishes, salads, and fruits. The atmosphere is relaxed yet genteel, and for those who don't want formal service: casual dress is permitted. Dinner features Creole dishes. Open daily: brunch 9am–3pm, dinner 5:30–10pm. Major credit cards.

Dominique's $$$$ *1001 Rue Toulouse at the Maison Dupuy Hotel, New Orleans 70112; Tel. (504) 522-8800.* Chef Dominique Macquet blends styles from his native Mauritius, his classical French training, and local ingredients at this award-winning restaurant. Open daily: breakfast 7am–10:30am, lunch 11:30am–2pm, dinner 6pm–10pm, brunch Saturday and Sunday 11:30am–2pm. Reservations recommended. Major credit cards.

Galatoire's $$$ *209 Bourbon Street, New Orleans 70130; Tel. (504) 525-2021; fax (504) 525-5900.* This small dining room, serving the best in French/Creole cuisine, has been family run since 1905. Tennessee Williams dined here regularly, as do many longstanding New Orleans locals, and the prices are not outrageous. Reservations only for parties of 8 and over, and only Tuesday–Thursday, so you may have to wait in line. Open Tuesday–Saturday 11:30am–9pm, Sunday noon–9pm. Major credit cards.

Johnny's Po-Boys $ *511 St. Louis Street, New Orleans 70130; Tel. (504) 524-8129.* This the place where locals come for their Po-boys, so it must be good. You can order almost any filling for your sandwich—accompanied by numerous salads and pickles. Open Monday–Friday 8am–4pm, Saturday–Sunday 9am–4pm. Cash only.

K-Paul's Louisiana Kitchen $$$$ *416 Chartres Street, New Orleans 70130; Tel. (504) 596-2530; fax (504) 943-2935; web site <www.kpauls.com>.* Home base of renowned Cajun chef Paul Prudhomme, whose TV programs and books have done much to publicize the cuisine countrywide. The Cajun food is good and spicy, but expect to wait in line for the popular first-floor tables. You can take his spices home with you. Open lunch Tuesday–Saturday 11:30am–2:30pm, dinner Monday–Saturday 5:30pm–10pm. Reservations for upstairs dining room only. Major credit cards.

Louisiana Pizza Kitchen $$ *95 French Market Place, New Orleans 70114; Tel. (504) 522-9500.* Nothing pretentious here, just great pizza, pastas, and salads in convivial surroundings. Open daily: lunch 11:30am–2:30pm, dinner 5:30pm–10pm. Major credit cards.

NOLA $$$–$$$$ *534 St. Louis Street, New Orleans 70130; Tel. (504) 522-6652; fax (504) 524-6178*. Celebrity chef Emeril Lagasse's less formal restaurant, NOLA has modern, bistro-style décor and serves world cuisine with a *nouvelle* twist. It also has a wood-burning stove for interesting pizzas and bread. Open lunch Monday–Saturday 11:30am–2pm; dinner Sunday–Thursday 6pm–10pm, Friday–Saturday 6pm–midnight. Major credit cards.

Père Antoine's $$–$$$ *741 Royal Street, New Orleans 70116; Tel. (504) 581-4478*. Perè Antoine's has a full Cajun/Creole menu without the silver service of the finer establishments, and thus at less cost. Service is good. Pretty corner setting allows those seated at the windows a good view. Open Monday–Friday 9am–midnight, Saturday–Sunday 8am–midnight. Cash only.

Royal Café $$–$$$ *700 Royal Street, New Orleans 70116; Tel. (504) 528-9086; fax (504) 528-9235; web site <www.royalcafe.com>*. Even if the Cajun/Creole food was relatively poor, the view from the wrought-iron balcony is one of the best in the French Quarter. As it is the food is good, the portions not overwhelming, and the service attentive. Open lunch Monday–Friday 11am–3pm, Saturday–Sunday 10am–3pm; dinner daily 6pm–10pm. Major credit cards.

Uptown

Bangkok Thai $$ *513 South Carrollton Avenue, New Orleans 70118; Tel. (504) 861-3932*. Good Thai food offered in two strengths, medium and spicy. The menu includes soups, Thai salads, and a range of curries, including a number of vegetarian dishes. Simple décor. Very near the universities, so much frequented by faculty and students. Only 150 ft (49 m) from the St. Charles streetcar line at its turn up Carrollton Avenue. Open lunch Monday–Friday 11:30am–2:30pm, dinner daily 5:30pm–10pm. Major credit cards.

Casamento's $ *4330 Magazine Street, New Orleans 70115; Tel. (504) 895-9761.* This is *the* place for oysters in New Orleans and well worth the trip out of the downtown area to try them. When it isn't oyster season, Casamento's is closed—they're that serious about what they do! Open mid September–mid June Tuesday–Sunday, 11:30am–1:30pm and 5:30pm–9:30pm. Cash only.

Commanders Palace $$$–$$$$$. *1403 Washington Avenue, New Orleans 70130; Tel. (504) 899-8221; fax (504) 981-5175; web site <www.commanderspalace.com>.* A visit to Commanders Palace is not just a meal, it's an event! The 1880s mansion setting in the Garden District is stunning enough, but the food and service tops the decor. Creole/French dishes; the desserts are amazing (bread pudding soufflé is the signature). Excellent wine list. Open daily: lunch Monday–Friday 11:30am–1:30pm, Saturday 11:30am–1:30pm, Sunday 10:30am–1:30pm; dinner 6pm–9:30pm. Reservations required. Dress code: no shorts, T-shirts, or jeans; jacket required at night. Major credit cards.

Deanie's Seafood Restaurant $$$ *1713 Lake Avenue, Metairie 70005; Tel. (800) 662-2586 (toll-free in US), (504) 834-1225; fax (504) 837-2166; web site <www.deanies.com>.* The name tells it like it is—seafood and lots of it. People come for a mess of crawfish, so it pays not to wear your best clothes. Set close to Lake Pontchartrain, this is a good choice after a long lakeside stroll. Open Sunday–Thursday 11am–10pm, Friday–Saturday 11am–11pm. Major credit cards.

Kelsey's $$$$ *3923 Magazine Street, New Orleans 70115; Tel. (504) 897-6722; fax (504) 897-6763.* Creole dishes served with a contemporary twist in this modern restaurant. The chef-owner worked for a number of years with Paul Prudhomme, but adds his own deft touch here. Open lunch Tuesday–Friday 11:30am–2pm; dinner Tuesday Thursday 5:30pm–9:30pm, Friday–Saturday 5:30pm–10pm. Reservations recommended. Major credit cards.

Martinique $$$ *5908 Magazine Street, New Orleans 70115; Tel. (504) 891-8495; fax (504) 861-0666.* This small restaurant with a wonderful courtyard and intimate dining room offers great food by French chef Hubert Sandot. Classic French dishes such as *coq au vin* are prepared with a few Creole touches. Open daily for dinner only 6pm–10pm. No reservations except for groups of six and over. Major credit cards.

Paella Restaurant $$$ *3637 Magazine Street, New Orleans 70115; Tel. (504) 895-0240; fax (504) 895-0244.* Spanish dishes, with paella a specialty. Tapas are also served if you'd like a light meal while antique hunting. There is a good range of Spanish wines and sherries to accompany the food. A few tables on the street for dining alfresco. Open Tuesday–Sunday lunch 11:30am–2:30pm, dinner 6pm–10pm. Major credit cards.

Ruth's Chris Steak House $$$$ *711 Broad Street, New Orleans 70119; Tel. (800) 544-0808 (toll-free in US), (504) 486-0810; fax (504) 528-9235; web site <www.ruthschris.com>.* This growing culinary empire started here—this is the original restaurant, and it's still serving some of the best steaks in New Orleans. Open Monday–Friday 11am–11pm, Saturday 4pm–11pm, Sunday 11:30am–10pm. Major credit cards.

Louisiana

Café des Amis $$–$$$ *140 East Bridge Street, Breaux Bridge 70517; Tel. (337) 332-5273; fax (337) 332-5273; web site*

<www.cafedesamis.com>. This airy, easygoing café-restaurant is a great place for food—Cajun dishes with lots of fresh ingredients—and it also serves as a gallery and meeting place for local artists. Great ambiance; not the slightest bit pretentious. Open Tuesday–Sunday 7:30am–10pm. Major credit cards.

Café Vermilionville $$$$ *1304 West Pinhook Road, Lafayette 70503; Tel. (337) 237-0100*. Set in a wonderful Acadian building circa 1800, this restaurant offers Cajun/Creole cuisine in more up-market surroundings than others outside New Orleans. White tablecloths and an excellent wine list accompany fresh seafood and meat dishes. The dining room overlooks a verdant courtyard. Open daily: lunch Monday–Friday 11am–2pm, dinner Monday–Saturday 5:30pm–10pm. Reservations recommended. Major credit cards.

Mulate's Cajun Restaurant $$–$$$ *325 Mills Avenue, Breaux Bridge 70517; Tel. (337) 332-4648*. Good Cajun food and music here, decorated like a huge bayou shack with checked tablecloths. Everyone gets on the dance floor, probably to work off the huge portions served here. All the usual Cajun dishes. Open Monday–Thursday 11am–10pm, Friday–Sunday 11am–10:30pm. Major credit cards.

Prejeans $$–$$$ *street address 3480 I49 North (2 miles north of I10); mailing address 3480 US Highway 167 North, Lafayette 70507; (318) 896-3247; fax (318) 896-3278; web site <www.prejeans.com>*. A huge stuffed alligator welcomes visitors to this award-winning Cajun restaurant. Live music every night. Large dining hall means lots of noise when the restaurant is busy. Food is typical Cajun but offers unusual dishes such as elk and buffalo. Open Monday–Thursday 11am–10pm, Thursday–Sunday 11am–11pm. Major credit cards.

INDEX